HEINEMANN GEOGRAPHY

Series editor: John Hopkin

People WEATHER & WATER

CELIA TIDMARSH   PAUL WEEDEN

HEINEMANN EDUCATIONAL

Heinemann Educational,
a division of Heinemann Educational Books Ltd.
Halley Court, Jordan Hill, Oxford OX2 8EJ

OXFORD LONDON EDINBURGH
MADRID ATHENS BOLOGNA PARIS
MELBOURNE SYDNEY AUCKLAND SINGAPORE
TOKYO IBADAN NAIROBI HARARE
GABORONE PORTSMOUTH NH (USA)

© Celia Tidmarsh and Paul Weeden 1991

First published 1991

British Library Cataloguing in Publication Data
Tidmarsh, Celia
  People, weather and water. – (Heinemann geography)
  1. Geography
  I. Title   II. Weeden, Paul
  910

  ISBN 0 435 35198 2

Designed and produced by Gecko Limited, Bicester, Oxon

Printed and bound in Spain by Mateu Cromo

Note to teachers

Details of National Curriculum Statements of Attainment covered are given on the pupil spreads; italics indicate partial coverage. A summary of the Statements of Attainment coverage is given in the matrix in the accompanying Teacher's Resource Pack.

Acknowledgements

The Publishers would like to thank the following for permission to reproduce photographs:

A.A. Picture Library, p.3 (G); The Bridgeman Art Library, p.46 (B); J. Allan Cash Ltd, pp. 6 (A), 9 (D), 11 (F), 17 (G, H), 26 (C, D), 31 (E, H, I), 33 (E), 39 (E, top, F), 40 (D); Celtic Picture Library, p.12 (C); China Photo Library, p.32 (C); D. Coombes, p.38 (B); FLPA/M.J. Thomas, p.12 (D); Greg Evans Picture Library, p.39 (E), 42 (A); S. Gaffney, p.43 (G); Gamma/Frank Spooner Pictures, p.13 (F); John Hopkin, pp. 4 (D), 8 (A, B), 29 (I); Hutchison Library, pp.7 (G), 24 (D), 33 (D, H), 36 (C), 41 (E); Frank Lane Picture Library, p.10 (B), 12 (D); Oxford Scientific Films, p.28 (G); P. Morris, p.43 (H); Science Photo Library, pp.17 (I), 24 (C), 31 (F), 46 (C); Still Moving Picture Co., p.34 (A, top right); University of Dundee Satellite Receiving Station, p.45 (E); Visual Publications, pp.15 (E), 16 (A, B, C, D), 20 (A, B, C), 23 (E, F, G), 35 (D, all), 38 (A); John Walmsey, p.17 (F).

All other photographs supplied by the authors.

Thanks are also due to the following for permission to reproduce copyright material: Australian Associated Press, p.13 (G); Rupert Besley, p.34 (B); Clacton Tourist Information Centre p.34 (A, bottom centre) Cosmoair Plc, p.6 (B, right, C, bottom left and middle right); Department of Transport, p.5 (F); Enterprise Holidays, p.6 (C, top left); *Falmouth Guide Ltd*, p.34 (A, left); *Geography Review*, p.24 (B); *The Guardian*, pp.10 (C), 43 (F), 44 (B); Hodder and Stoughton, p.47 (F), which appeared in *The Greenhouse Effect* by Stewart Boyle and John Ardill; Horizon Holidays p.7 (G); *The Independent*, p.11 (E, G, H); Intasun p.6 (C, middle left); Meteorological Office, pp.44 (C), 45 (D), reproduced with the permission of the Controller of Her Majesty's Stationery Office; Oxfam, p.10 (D); Scottish Tourist Board, p.34 (A, top right text only); Thomson Holidays Ltd, p.6 (B, left, C, top left, bottom left); *The Times* p.12 (A, B);
The Publishers have made every attempt to contact the correct copyright holders. If any material has been incorrectly attributed, the Publishers would be pleased to make the necessary arrangements at the earliest opportunity.

Contents

Weather, water and our lives
How weather affects our lives	4
Mediterranean sunshine	6
Global weather and climate	8
Dramatic weather events	10
Flooding	12

Investigating weather and water
Investigating the water cycle	14
Measuring the weather	16
Looking locally	18
Clouding over	20
Why does it rain?	22
Winding it up	24

Water and the landscape
Investigating water movements	26
Processes in river channels	28
River valley landforms	30
River basins	32

Weather and climate around the world
Weather differences in the British Isles	34
Latitude, land and sea	36
The spinning earth	38
Hot desert climate	40
Cold forest climate	42

Future weather and climate
Forecasting the weather	44
How the climate changes	46
Glossary	48

How weather affects our lives

A *In what ways does the weather affect your everyday life?*

B Snow

C Rain

D Sunshine

BLIZZARDS HIT THE NORTH

PHEW! WHAT A SCORCHER!

Hosepipe ban begins

STORMS & GALES BRING CHAOS

The big freeze continues . . .

RAIN STOPS PLAY

E *Weather in the headlines*

F *Weather hazards for cars*

G *Talking weather*

Speech bubbles:
- It's freezing!
- The wind goes right through you!
- THERE'S NOT A CLOUD IN THE SKY.
- I'M BOILING!
- It's really hot and sticky. We need a thunderstorm to clear the air.
- We got caught in a shower.

1. Think back to yesterday and describe how the weather affected you. Use A to help you.

2. For each of the photos (B, C and D) say what would be a good way to spend each day.

3. Using E write a newspaper story to go with each headline.

4. **a** What weather hazards do the road signs warn of?
   b List as many ways as you can think of in which the weather affects transport and travel (F).

5. Choose two of the quotes in G and draw cartoons to go with them.

Mediterranean sunshine

A At the Spanish seaside

B Holiday brochures give us weather data . . .

HOLIDAY WEATHER
AVERAGE MONTHLY TEMPERATURES (°F)

	Mar	Apr	May	Jun	Jul	Aug	Sep	Oct	Nov
C. del Sol	64	69	74	80	84	85	81	74	66
London	50	55	63	68	72	70	66	57	50

AVERAGE HRS OF SUNSHINE

	Mar	Apr	May	Jun	Jul	Aug	Sep	Oct	Nov
C. del Sol	7	8	10	11	11	11	9	7	6
London	3	6	7	7	7	6	5	3	2

Average Daily Max. Temp.

Apr	May	Jun	Jul	Aug	Sep	Oct
9	10	11	12	11	8	7
5	6	7	6	6	5	3

Average Hours of Sunshine
■ Resort □ London

ADVANTAGES
Aptly named the Sunshine Coast, the Costa del Sol was made to be a holiday centre!

OUR OPINION
Sun and fun all the way! With Benidorm as the focus, the Costa Blanca has made its name as one of the liveliest holiday spots in the whole of Europe, with supreme sandy beaches and glorious summer weather.

YOUR RESORT
'An area tailor-made for the British holidaymaker, with great beaches, good food and excellent entertainment at value-for-money prices.'
In the brilliant glare of the midday sun Spain's 'White Coast' looks, and is, hot. With one of the best sunshine records in the Mediterranean, and a backdrop of rocky mountains which reflect the rays, there can be very few better places for that seaside tanning holiday.

This is Spain's popular southern coast, the Costa del Sol, famed for its 320 sunny days a year and miles of sandy beaches. As a result of these mouthwatering attractions, a whole new holiday world has developed along the Mediterranean shoreline facing Africa.

The radiant Costa Blanca lies half way down Spain's Mediterranean coast beside an array of outstanding beaches. Its main resort, Benidorm, is the country's top summer destination and you'll soon realise why. For a start there's its climate. Hot, sunny, but never oppressive, thanks to the bone dry air and high season breezes.

Sunshine, bright lights and superb sandy beaches, blue-green seas, orange groves and picturesque villages, mountains, old fortresses and starry evenings – all part of the Costa Blanca's particular charm.

The weather is exceptional. In spring it's warm and sunny and the colours of citrus fruits, flowers and blossom splash the countryside. In summer it's gloriously hot and in autumn the balmy days merge slowly into each other. This is perhaps why the Costa Blanca has become so incredibly popular with holidaymakers.

C . . . and descriptions

D The location of the popular Costas in Spain

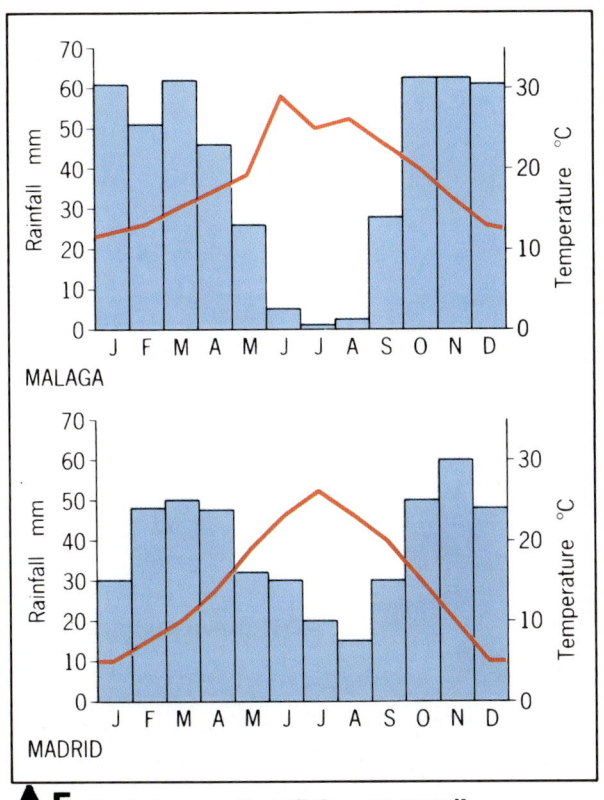

E *Spain has weather all the year round!*

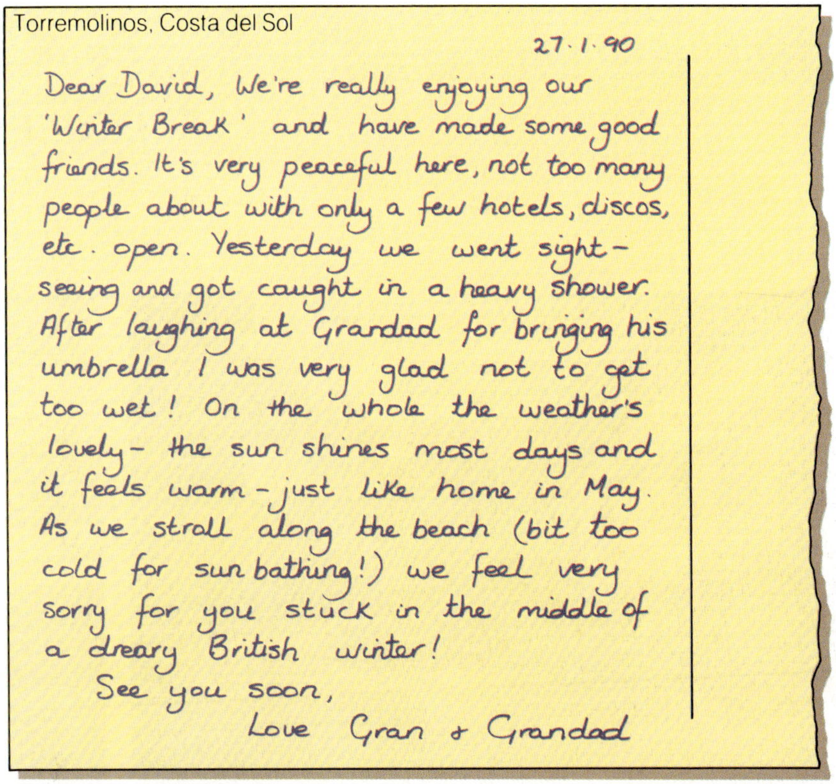

MALAGA

MADRID

F *Winter postcard from Spain*

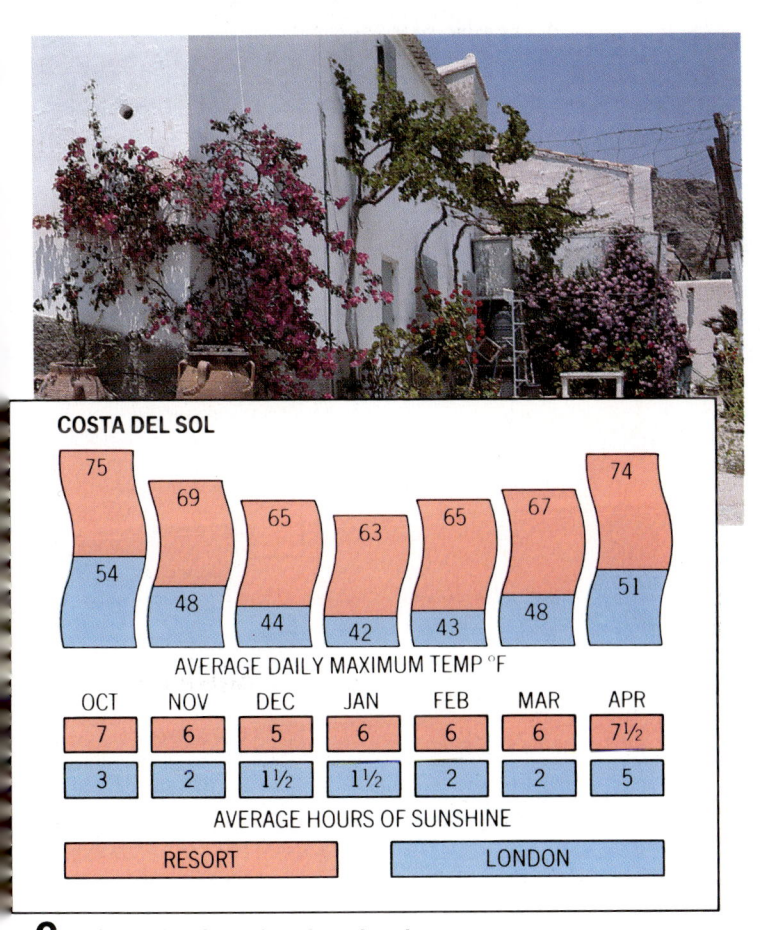

Torremolinos, Costa del Sol
27.1.90

Dear David, We're really enjoying our 'Winter Break' and have made some good friends. It's very peaceful here, not too many people about with only a few hotels, discos, etc. open. Yesterday we went sight-seeing and got caught in a heavy shower. After laughing at Grandad for bringing his umbrella I was very glad not to get too wet! On the whole the weather's lovely - the sun shines most days and it feels warm - just like home in May. As we stroll along the beach (bit too cold for sun bathing!) we feel very sorry for you stuck in the middle of a dreary British winter!
See you soon,
Love Gran & Grandad

COSTA DEL SOL

AVERAGE DAILY MAXIMUM TEMP °F

	OCT	NOV	DEC	JAN	FEB	MAR	APR
Resort	75	69	65	63	65	67	74
London	54	48	44	42	43	48	51

AVERAGE HOURS OF SUNSHINE

	OCT	NOV	DEC	JAN	FEB	MAR	APR
Resort	7	6	5	6	6	6	7½
London	3	2	1½	1½	2	2	5

G *Information from the winter brochures*

1. **a** Choose either the Costa Blanca or the Costa del Sol. Make a list of the information we are given about the weather for that particular area.
   b Join up with someone who has looked at the other area and compare your lists. Are there any differences between them?
   c How would *you* choose which of the two areas to visit?

2. Look carefully at E, F and G and say why David's grandparents have gone to Torremolinos for their winter holiday instead of to a British holiday **resort**. (Pages 34 and 35 will help you with information on British holiday resorts for a more detailed answer.)

   You could present your answer in the form of a table:

	Sunshine	Rainfall	Temperature
Torremolinos			
British seaside resort			

Gg 2/4a, 6b, 7d; Gg 3/5b, 6b

Global weather and climate

A A village house in Barbados

- Pitched roof – to cope with the heavy rainfall
- Louvred shutters – to keep out the sun and let in the breeze
- Trees and vegetation – to provide shade around the house

B A village on Mikonos, Greece

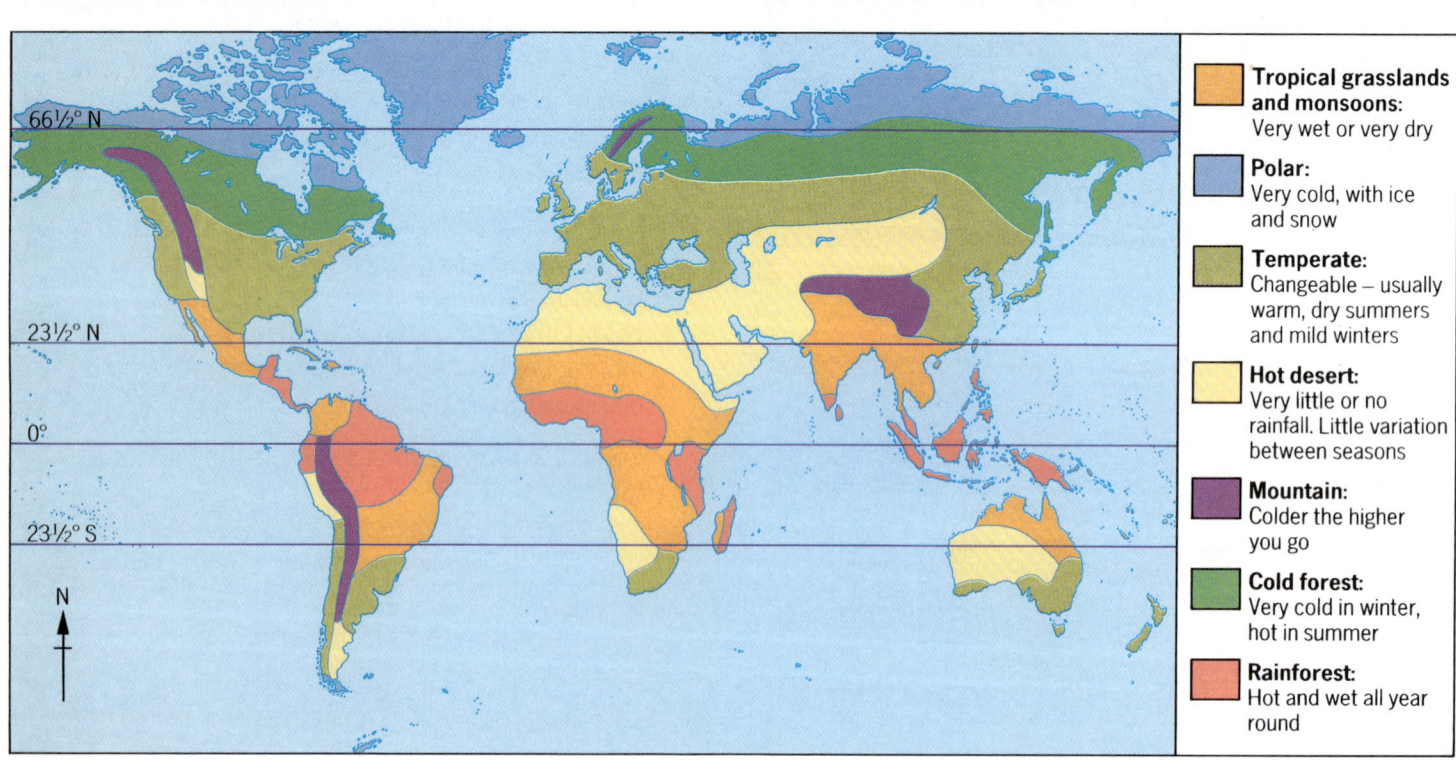

C Climates of the world

- **Tropical grasslands and monsoons:** Very wet or very dry
- **Polar:** Very cold, with ice and snow
- **Temperate:** Changeable – usually warm, dry summers and mild winters
- **Hot desert:** Very little or no rainfall. Little variation between seasons
- **Mountain:** Colder the higher you go
- **Cold forest:** Very cold in winter, hot in summer
- **Rainforest:** Hot and wet all year round

A E *Where do they come from?*

D *Clothes for a cold climate*

F *The climate affects what can be grown*

Items of Food	Temperature	Rainfall	Other climatic conditions	Examples of where produced
Tomatoes	Mild in winter	Moderate	Early spring. Little or no frost. Often grown in glasshouses.	Channel Isles
Oranges	Hot in summer, warm in winter	Wet winters	—	Spain, Israel
Tea	Average monthly temps at least 18°C during nine-month growing season	Between 1500 and 7500 mm during year	High humidity with morning mist or dew	Sri Lanka, Tanzania
Grapes	Summer temps not below 20°C	Long dry period for ripening	—	Italy, California (USA)
Cauliflower	Mild in winter	Moderate	Early spring. Little or no frost	South-west England
Wheat	Growing season temperatures of 15–21°C for about three months. Warm dry period for ripening	380–900 mm during year	—	Canada, central USA
Rice	Minimum temps of 21°C for about five months followed by dry sunny period for ripening	Over 2000 mm during year	—	Parts of India, China
Coffee	Average monthly temps of 21–26°C	1700 mm during year. Dry season for picking	High humidity	Brazil, Angola
Bananas	Warmth. Average temps of 21–26°C. Lots of sun	Annual rainfall 2000 mm	Lack of strong winds after the fruit has ripened	Jamaica, Costa Rica

1 **a** Look at photos A and B. In what ways have the houses been built to cope with hot weather?
   b Use map C to decide what types of **climate** photos A and B show. Check your answers in an atlas.

2 **a** In which climate does the person in photo D live?
   b How do you think her house might be adapted to the cold climate?

3 **a** Choose five of the food items from E and F. Mark the countries they come from on a world map.
   b Use C and an atlas to find out which climates these foods are grown in.

Gg 1/4e; Gg 3/3a, 5b, 6b

Dramatic weather events

A The path of Hurricane Hugo through the Caribbean

B What Hurricane Hugo left behind

Hugo descends on Puerto Rico
Martin Walker in Washington and Mark Wilson in Barbados

Hurricane Hugo battered the 3.3 million people of the island of Puerto Rico yesterday with winds of up to 125 mph.

The storm, which had killed nine people in its crawl across the eastern Caribbean, was moving at 8 to 10 mph, while the winds whipping around the storm centre uprooted trees, cut telephone and power lines, and ripped the roofs from houses.

More than 10,000 people were evacuated to government shelters, but there were no immediate reports of casualties on Puerto Rico, which had 24 hours to prepare for the region's worst hurricane in 10 years.

The eye of the hurricane was some 20 miles off Puerto Rico's north coast yesterday evening, raising hopes that the island could be spared the worst of the storm. Its trail across the island had slowed Hugo's winds from their earlier peaks of 140 mph.

The first two planes of doctors and medical supplies arrived in the ravaged French island of Guadeloupe yesterday, where Hugo left five dead, more than 80 injured and 10,000 homeless.

'There is nothing left of St Francois,' said the mayor of Guadeloupe's St Francois tourist resort. 'Aside from a few houses, almost all the rest are destroyed, and hotels very seriously damaged.'

On Dominica, the storms were still washing away the dirt roads needed to get what is left of the country's crucial banana crop to the ports.

The damage to communications and radio antennae delayed reports of the hurricane's impact on other Caribbean islands.

In Montserrat, the hospital was badly hit, and the roof blown off the only power station. The airport is closed, and reported to be badly damaged. The airport was still closed on St Kitts late yesterday, but Antigua and Dominica were re-opened, largely to facilitate the arrival of aid planes.

C News of Hurricane Hugo

D Appeal for help ▷

HURRICANE HUGO RAVAGES CARIBBEAN

- **Trail of devastation** left by most powerful hurricane to hit Eastern Caribbean for a decade.
- **65,000 people left homeless** and hundreds injured.
- **Destruction of crops and farmland** threatens fragile economies of region.
- **Dominica has lost 80% of its vital banana crop,** dirt roads have been washed away. Oxfam's main priority is to help with long-term recovery for Dominican poor.

Oxfam's emergency relief work is helping poor people in Mozambique, Sudan, Ethiopia, Uganda — and now in the Eastern Caribbean.

YOUR HELP IS URGENTLY NEEDED.

Please send your donation for Oxfam's emergency work to:

OXFAM

Oxfam,
Room OB55,
274 Banbury Rd,
Oxford OX2 7DZ.

E *Path of the storm, 25 January 1990 and some of the damage it caused*

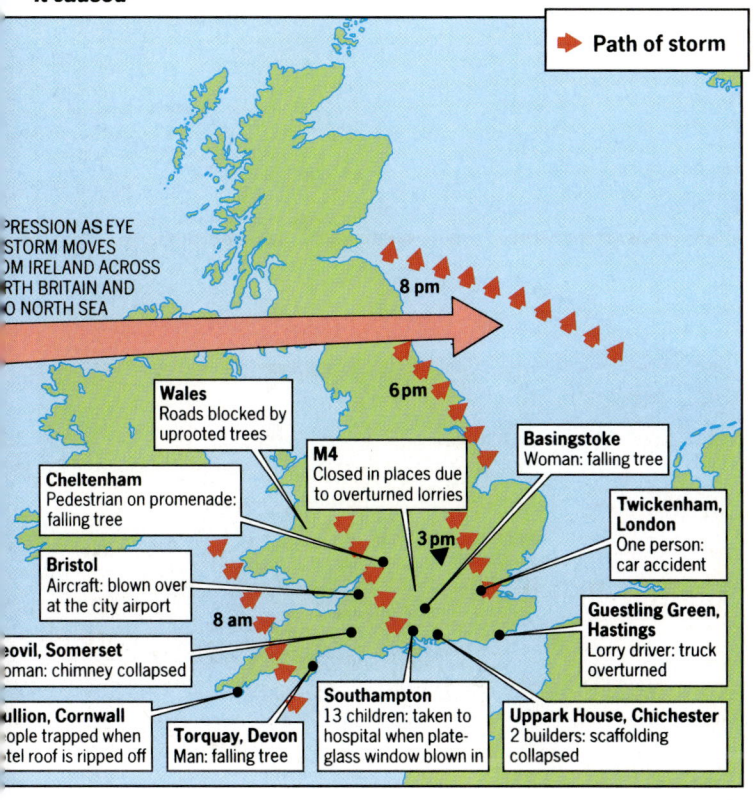

➡ Path of storm

DEPRESSION AS EYE OF STORM MOVES FROM IRELAND ACROSS NORTH BRITAIN AND TO NORTH SEA

8 pm
6 pm
3 pm
8 am

Wales Roads blocked by uprooted trees

Cheltenham Pedestrian on promenade: falling tree

Bristol Aircraft: blown over at the city airport

Yeovil, Somerset Woman: chimney collapsed

Mullion, Cornwall People trapped when hotel roof is ripped off

Torquay, Devon Man: falling tree

M4 Closed in places due to overturned lorries

Southampton 13 children: taken to hospital when plate-glass window blown in

Basingstoke Woman: falling tree

Twickenham, London One person: car accident

Guestling Green, Hastings Lorry driver: truck overturned

Uppark House, Chichester 2 builders: scaffolding collapsed

F *Luckily no one was hurt when this tree was torn up*

"IT'S NOT RAIN – IT'S PEOPLE IN THE CLAIMS DEPARTMENT WEEPING"

INSURANCE

H *A cartoonist's view*

▼ G *News of the violent storm which hit Britain on 25 January 1990*

32 killed in storm devastation

By Phil Reeves and James Cusick

AT LEAST 32 people died as hurricane force winds swept across southern Britain yesterday, leaving a trail of disruption and damage estimated at many hundreds of millions of pounds.

Buildings were blown down, trees ripped off their roots, and roofs torn off as the second severe storm to affect Britain in three years crossed the country from west to east.

Large areas were without electricity, telephone services were disrupted and London ground to a virtual standstill as all public transport was thrown into chaos.

The Government announced emergency funds would be given to local authorities in the worst-affected areas, although the amount was not specified.

Road, rail, sea and air travel was severely disrupted for much of the day, by winds gusting at more than 100mph. Dozens of vehicles were blown over – one policeman said they were "thrown about like toys".

The South-east, West Country, Wales and the Midlands were the worst affected areas, although there were heavy snow and blizzards in Scotland and northern England. Thousands of homes suffered power cuts.

With fallen trees and electricity cables damaged in the storm, it was estimated last night that more than half a million homes were without power. Telephone cables and services were also badly hit in Kent, East Sussex, Surrey and Hampshire.

Early estimates of damage were being put at more than £800m. Some London insurance offices were receiving 150 claim calls an hour yesterday evening.

---

1. Study the information on these two pages. Use the following headings to draw up a table to compare the case studies of the Caribbean countries with Britain.

    What happened?
    Damage caused to property.
    Effects on people.
    Paying for the repairs.

    Include how long it lasted, the size of area if affected, the wind speed, etc.

Flooding

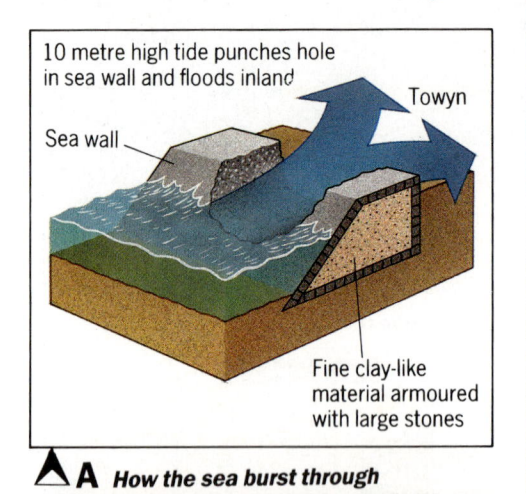

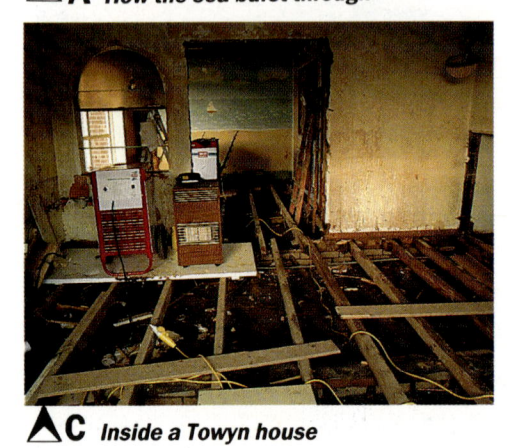

A How the sea burst through
10 metre high tide punches hole in sea wall and floods inland
Sea wall — Towyn — Fine clay-like material armoured with large stones

B The area flooded – Tuesday 27 February

Map legend: Sea; Low-lying land; Higher ground (above 15 m); Housing; Sea wall; Railway; Road.

Locations shown: Rhyl, A548, Sea wall, Breached sea wall, Pensarn station, Pensarn, Abergele, Belgrano, Towyn, Kinmel Bay, River Clwyd, Flooded area, A547, Bodelwyddan Castle.

C Inside a Towyn house

D Repairing the sea wall

Flooding is always news. People's lives, homes and possessions are damaged or destroyed. In February 1990 the people of Towyn, Clwyd, North Wales had their lives shattered when the sea wall was broken (A–E).

E Diary of the Towyn flood

26 Monday 160 km/h winds and very high tides breach sea wall at Towyn (A). Four hundred people are evacuated.

27 Tuesday High tides and storm winds bring more flooding, sea wall breach is widened to 200 metres. One thousand people are now in emergency accommodation.

28 Wednesday Storms continue to batter Britain. Villages of Pensarn and Kinmel Bay are evacuated (B). Two thousand people are now homeless.

1 Thursday Flood zone is now 8 km wide and stretches 4 km inland. Prince and Princess of Wales visit victims at the emergency centre. The Towyn disaster fund reaches £40 000.

2 Friday A few people are allowed back to Towyn to see their wrecked homes. Some weep as they walk through sewage and sl... to inspect the damage. Disaster fund has reached £100 000.

3 Saturday Angry and bitter people ask 'why did it have to happen?' as they return to view the filth and destruction (C).

4 Sunday Emergency workers have worked around the cl... since Thursday dumping 60 000 tonnes of rock and cement into the sea wall breach (D).

5 Monday Police maintain an **exclusion zone** while safe... checks on electricity supplies are carried out. A total of 28... homes in Towyn, Kinmel Bay and Pensarn have been floode...

Rivers can flood after heavy rainfall (F). If too much water gets into the river at one time it will overflow its banks and flood low-lying land nearby.

Heavy rain brings floods to eastern Australia

In April 1990 the highest rainfall recorded in 100 years fell over eastern Australia. River flooding destroyed homes and cut off many small communities (F, G). An area the size of Britain was submerged by a huge inland sea 800 kilometres wide. Damage was estimated at tens of millions of Australian dollars. The Royal Australian Airforce dropped food for people who were cut off and evacuated people to Longreach and Brisbane.

F Flooding in Australia

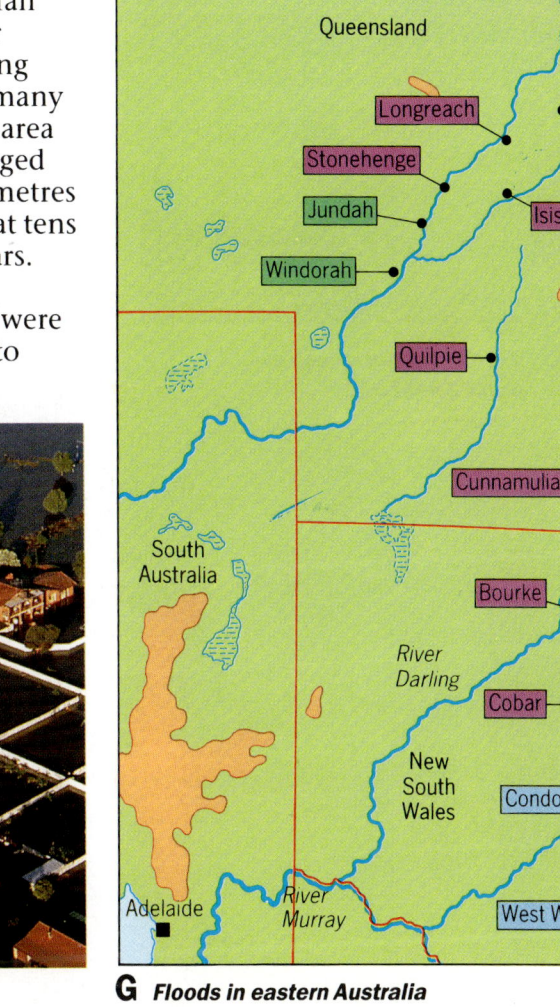

G Floods in eastern Australia

Key:
- Cut off, water rising
- Cut off, water stable
- Cut off, water falling
- Water rising
- Water stable
- Mountain

1. Make a report on the Towyn floods. Include details of what caused them, what the effects were, and how people dealt with the disaster. Illustrate your report with pictures or maps. You could present your work as a newspaper page, police report or letter from a local householder.

2. Describe or sketch the scene in photo F.

3. On a copy of map G:
   a Label details of flood levels. You will have to make a key to show whether river levels were rising, steady (stable) or falling.
   b Underline all the towns that were cut off. Use this information to map the area of the inland sea that formed.
   c What evidence is there that the flooding was moving south?

4. You are organizing the evacuation of people from the flooded towns. Your base is in Brisbane and you have three helicopters.
   - Plan your routes.
   - Work out the distances each helicopter will have to fly.

Gg 1/4b, 5d, 6a; Gg 3/5c, 6g   13

Investigating the water cycle

The water cycle is essential for life on earth. Energy from the sun **evaporates** water from the oceans and land. This **water vapour condenses** to form clouds (C), which are blown along by the wind (D). The vapour then falls back to the ground as rain (E), hail or snow. This is called **precipitation**. The water either travels over the land in rivers (F) (**runoff**) or sinks into the ground (**infiltration**). Eventually most water will return to the sea (A).

▽D *(For more about winds see pages 20–21)*

▲C *(For more about clouds see pages 16–17)*

▲B *(For more about measuring the weather see pages 16–17)*

Evaporation from sea

Sea

Condensation

Transpiration from plants

Evaporation from rivers and lakes

Runoff in rivers

A *The water cycle*

14

▲ E *(For more about rainfall see pages 22–24)*

Air	0.001%
Ice	1.9%
Lakes and rivers	0.01%
Oceans	97.579%
Soil	0.01%
Underground	0.5%

▲ G **Where is the world's water?**

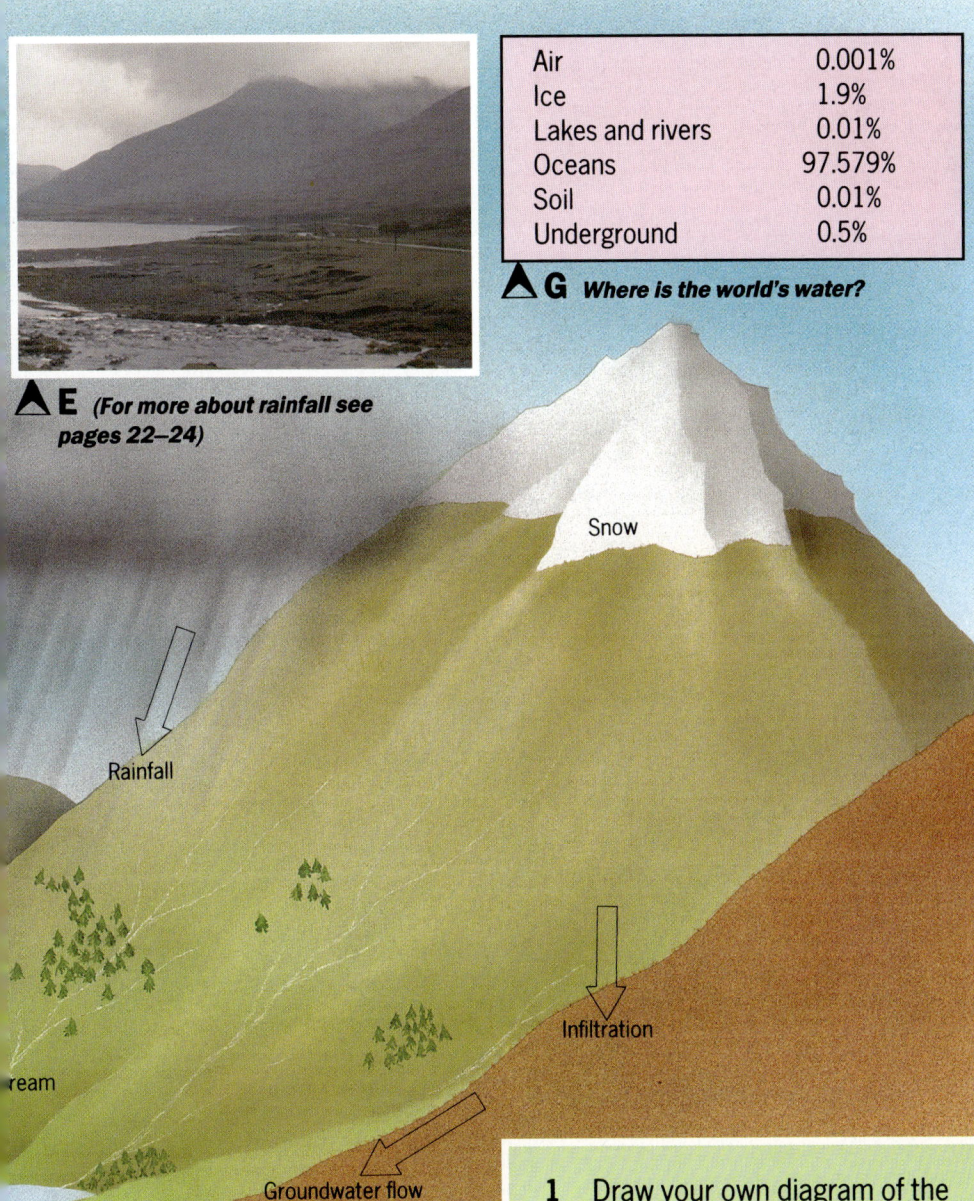

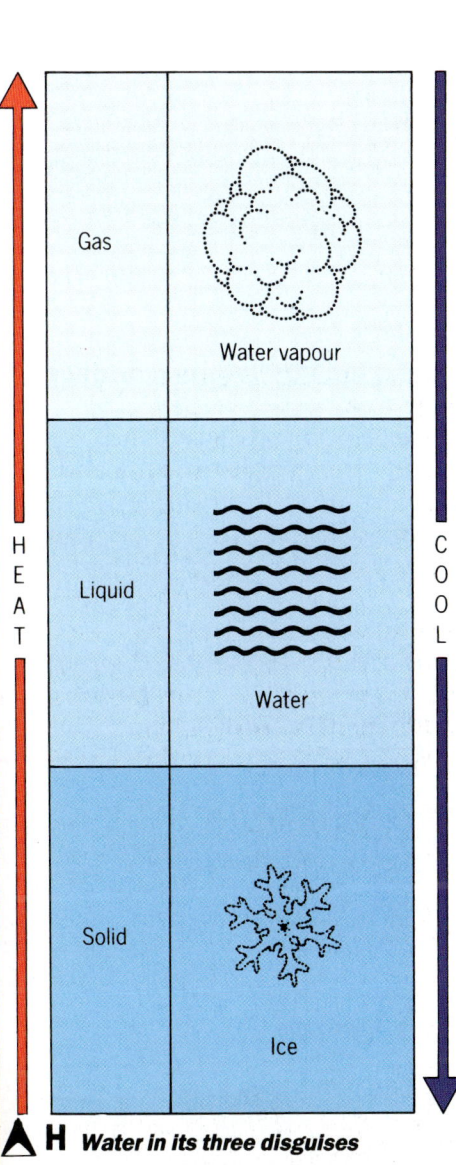

Snow

Rainfall

Infiltration

Groundwater flow

Stream

HEAT → COOL

Gas — Water vapour

Liquid — Water

Solid — Ice

▲ H **Water in its three disguises**

▲ F *(For more about rivers see pages 26–28)*

1. Draw your own diagram of the water cycle.

2. Explain in your own words how the water cycle works and why it is vital to life on earth.

3. Pictures C, D, E and F show parts of the water cycle that can be investigated.
   a In pairs suggest what could be observed or measured in each photograph.
   b How could the features you have suggested be measured?

4. Water occurs in three disguises.
   a What are these disguises?
   b Find out the temperatures at which water changes from:
   • solid to liquid
   • liquid to gas

5. Copy and complete this table.

Where the world's water is stored			%
Most	1	Oceans	97.579
	2		
	3		
	4		
	5		
Least	6	Air	0.001
Total			100.000

Gg 3/3b, 6c 15

Measuring the weather

People often observe and comment on the weather in everday conversation or in diaries and letters. Some people measure and record the weather using instruments. These accurate weather records are used in forecasting weather, describing different **climates** around the world and predicting climatic change. Some of the instruments used are shown on these pages (A, B, C, D).

A Wind-vane

B Anemometer

Tuesday April 7

There was a south-westerly gale today which made it very wet, but warmer than last week. I had to stay inside all day. The barometer is going up, so it may be drier tomorrow.

E Weather diary

C Rain-gauge

D Barometer

1 **a** The five photos A–D and F show instruments used to measure five elements of the weather. What are the five elements of the weather? Use diary E to help give you ideas.

b What details does the diary give about the elements? What words could you use to describe each element?

c Match the five elements of the weather listed on the right with the pictures of the instruments used to measure them.
- Wind direction
- Wind speed
- Rainfall
- Pressure
- Temperature

16

Temperature is measured using a **thermometer** (F). The highest (maximum) and lowest (minimum) temperatures are recorded for each day. These temperatures are always measured in the shade, as are the temperatures given in forecasts. Thermometers at weather stations are kept in a **thermometer screen** (G). This shades them from the sun.

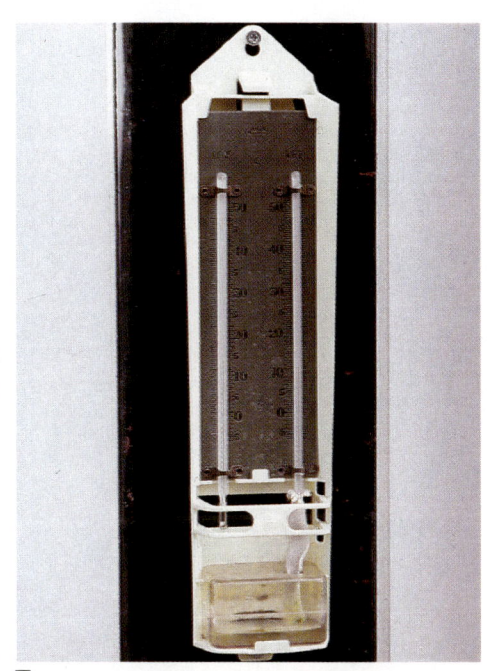

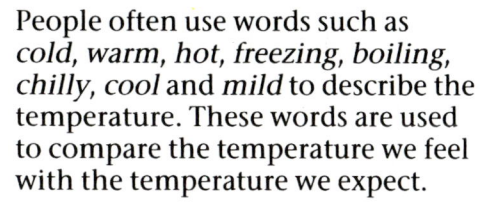

F Maximum and minimum thermometer

G Thermometer screen

H Sunbathing +28°C

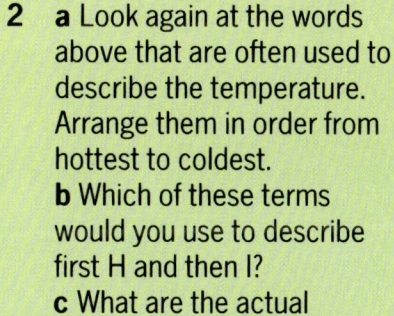

I In the snow −4°C

People often use words such as *cold, warm, hot, freezing, boiling, chilly, cool* and *mild* to describe the temperature. These words are used to compare the temperature we feel with the temperature we expect.

2 **a** Look again at the words above that are often used to describe the temperature. Arrange them in order from hottest to coldest.
b Which of these terms would you use to describe first H and then I?
c What are the actual temperatures in H and I

3 **a** How would you describe the temperature in your classroom?
b How would the people in H describe the temperature?
c Find out the actual temperature in the classroom.

4 **a** How would you describe the temperature outside?
b How would the people in I describe the temperature?
c Find out the actual temperature outside.

Looking locally

Temperature, sunshine and wind speed can vary at different places around a building. Pupils in a school learn which are the warmest, sunniest or calmest places to sit. These local differences are known as **microclimate**

B Location 1

C Location 2

D Location 3

E Location 4

A Map of Brislington School, Bristol

Key:
- School buildings
- Concrete
- Grass
- Photographer
- Trees

1 Study map A and photographs B, C, D and E. The photographs were all taken at midday on a sunny September day during lunchtime. The temperature was 23 °C, the wind was a light air (force 1) from the south west.

a For each photograph decide in which direction the photographer was looking.
b How many pupils can you see in each photo?
c Which location is most popular?
d Where are the best locations for: sunbathing; playing games; reading?

Aspect

As the earth rotates around its axis the sun appears to move. Diagram F shows the position of the sun at different times of the day.

You have probably noticed that some classrooms are hot and sunny while others are cold. This is because of the direction the windows face (**aspect**). Plan G shows a school block with four classrooms, each with two windows. Table H shows which windows will be facing the sun at different times of the day.

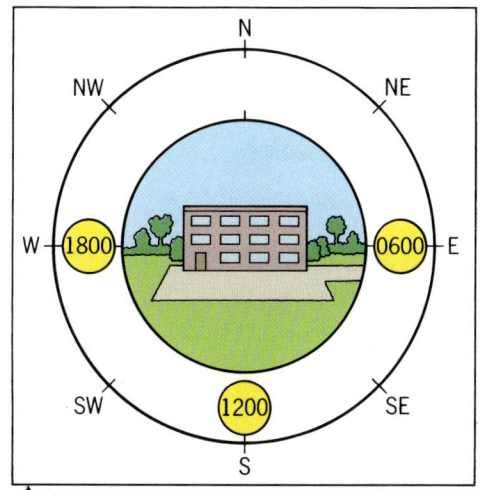

F *The position of the sun at different times of the day*

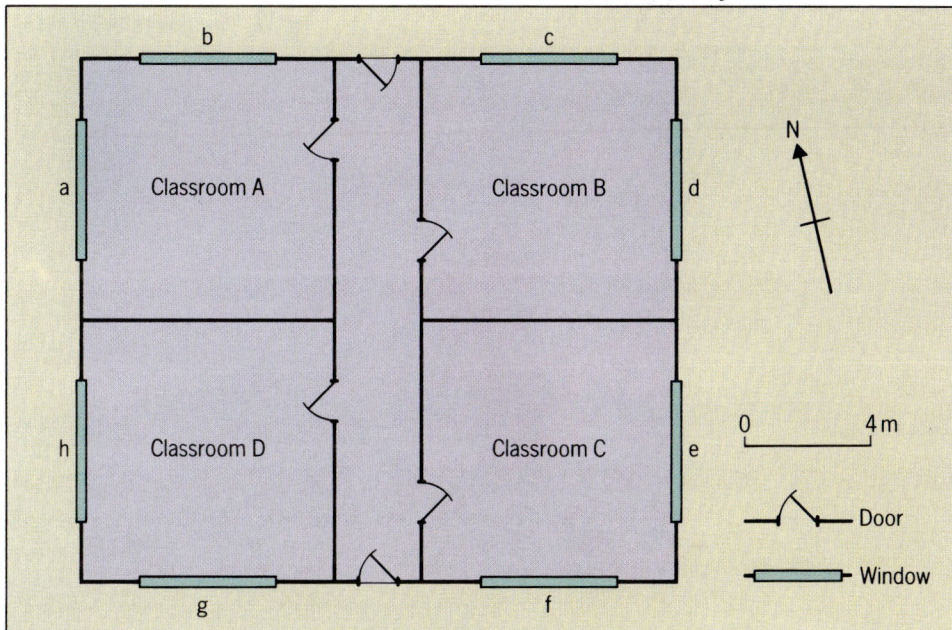

G *Plan of four classrooms in a school block*

H *Sunshine in each classroom during a sunny day*

2. Look at F. From which direction will the sun be shining at
   a 0900 hours?
   b 1500 hours?

3. Look at plan G.
   a Match up statements i–iv below with the correct classrooms A–D.
      i Sun all day
      ii Sun in the morning
      iii Sun in the afternoon
      iv Sun most of the day
   b Which classroom will be coldest in winter?
   c Which classroom will be hottest in summer?

4. Collect information about your school.
   a Which parts are sunny in the morning?
   b Which parts are sunny in the afternoon?
   c Where are the most popular places outside at lunchtime?
   d Is this because of the microclimate or are there other reasons?
   e Keep a record of sunshine in your classrooms like the table below.

Time of day (lesson)	Room	Sunny	Aspect of Windows
0930 (1)	M2	Yes	SE

Gg 1/3b, 4d, 6b; Gg 3/4a

Clouding over

▲A

▲B

▲C

▼D Ten major cloud types

What is a cloud?

A **cloud** is made up of millions of water droplets which are so small they float in the air. Flying through a cloud is like being in fog.

What cloud types are there?

There are three main cloud families – **stratus, cumulus** and **cirrus** (D). Clouds are classified by height and shape (E).

The word *alto* is added to cloud names to describe clouds that are high in the sky, e.g. *alto-cumulus*.

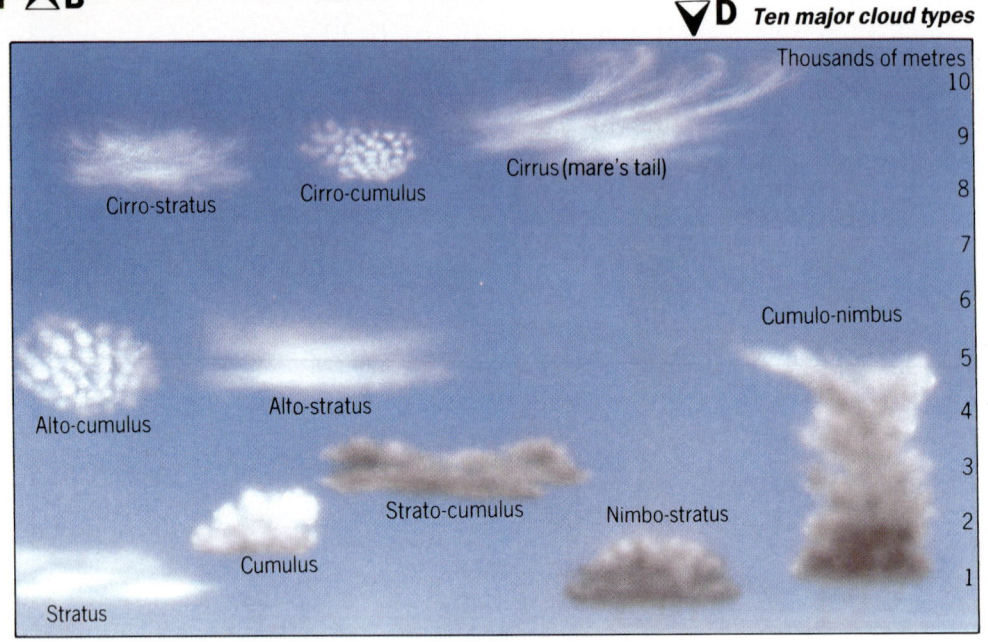

Cirro-stratus · Cirro-cumulus · Cirrus (mare's tail) · Alto-cumulus · Alto-stratus · Cumulo-nimbus · Cumulus · Strato-cumulus · Nimbo-stratus · Stratus

Thousands of metres: 10, 9, 8, 7, 6, 5, 4, 3, 2, 1

Cloud type	Cloud shape	Cloud height
Cirrus	Heaped-up cotton wool	Low in the sky
Cumulus	Layers	Very high
Stratus	Wispy thread	Low bases but tops may rise high

◄E A student's jumbled up list of information about clouds

What weather do clouds bring?

Many clouds do not bring rain. Rain clouds are dark grey in colour and are called **nimbus** clouds. *Cumulo-nimbus* clouds bring showers. *Nimbo-stratus* clouds bring prolonged drizzle or rain.

1 Match up each of the photographs A, B and C with the correct clouds in diagram D.
2 A student has made three lists of information about clouds (E). However, the lists are jumbled up. Sort them so that the cloud types match the descriptions of shape and height. Write them out in the right order.
3 Look out of the window. What cloud types can you see?

How much cloud is there?

We estimate how much cloud cover there is by dividing the sky into eighths (F). If half the sky is covered with cloud there is $\frac{4}{8}$ cloud cover.

How do clouds form?

Clouds of steam are sometimes created in a kitchen if a kettle or saucepan is left to boil (G). So much water is **evaporated** that the air becomes **saturated** with **water vapour** which **condenses** to form water droplets. Condensation is most common where there is a cold surface or particle for the water to collect on.

In a cloud, water droplets form when the air cools enough for some water vapour to condense on to minute specks of dust and salt in the air.

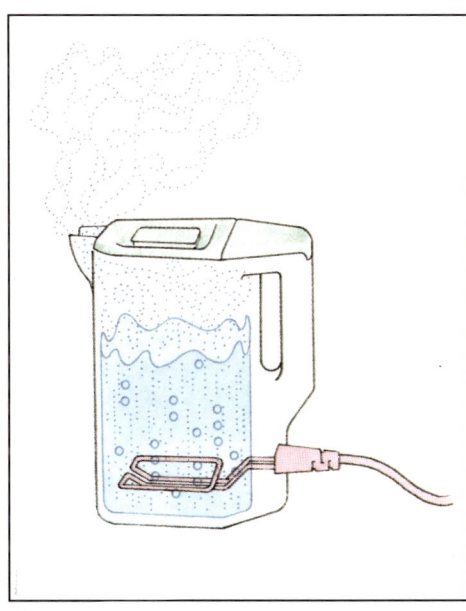

The amount of cloud in the sky, shown by the number of eighths of the sky covered

| No clouds | 1 or less | 2 | 3 | 4 | 5 | 6 | 7 | 8 | Sky can't be seen |

▲ F **Cloud cover symbols**

▼ H **Conditions in a cloud on a summer's day**

Enlarged view of ice particles

Nucleus

Enlarged view of water droplets

Salt nucleus   Dust nucleus

Saturated air

Unsaturated air

G **Boiling kettle**

People who fly hot air balloons find that the temperature falls as they rise (H). As it gets colder, air can hold less water vapour and becomes saturated so water droplets form. The height at which this happens is called the **condensation level**.

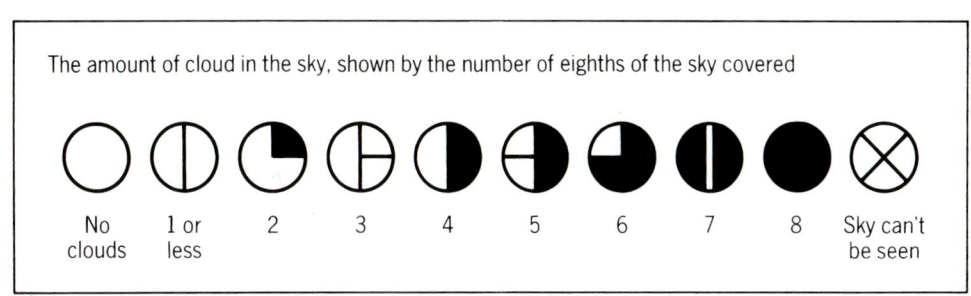

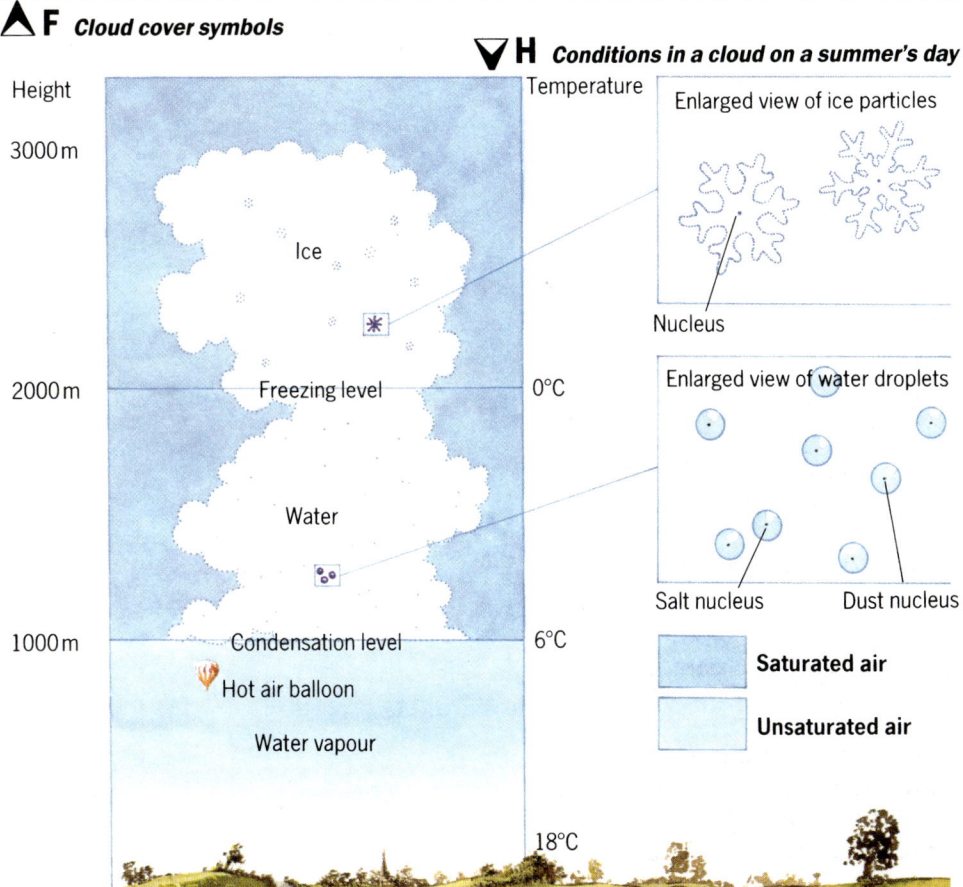

4 Look at photograph A.
 a Estimate in eighths how much of the sky is covered.
 b How much does the cloud cover symbol suggest is covered?
 c Do your answers to **a** and **b** match up?

5 Look at photographs B and C. Estimate in eighths how much of the sky is covered and use F to draw the correct cloud cover symbols.

6 Look out of the window. What is the cloud cover?

7 a Draw a sketch of the boiling kettle (G). Add these labels to your picture: water vapour (gas), water (liquid), evaporation, condensation.
 b Why don't the droplets in the cloud of steam fall to the ground?

8 Describe a journey in a hot air balloon up through the cloud. Use diagram H to help you.

Gg 1/4d; Gg 3/6a, 6c   21

Why does it rain?

Rain in Britain

Britain is famous for its rain but some places are wetter than others (A and B). Rain occurs when moist air is forced to rise (E, F and G).

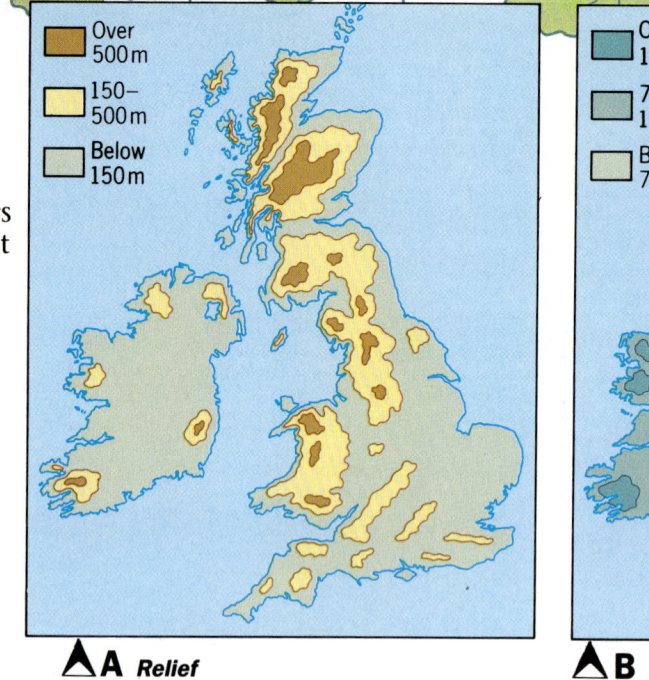

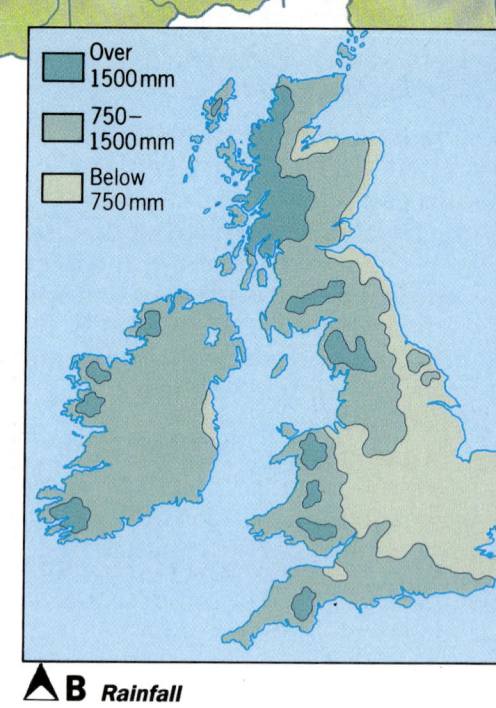

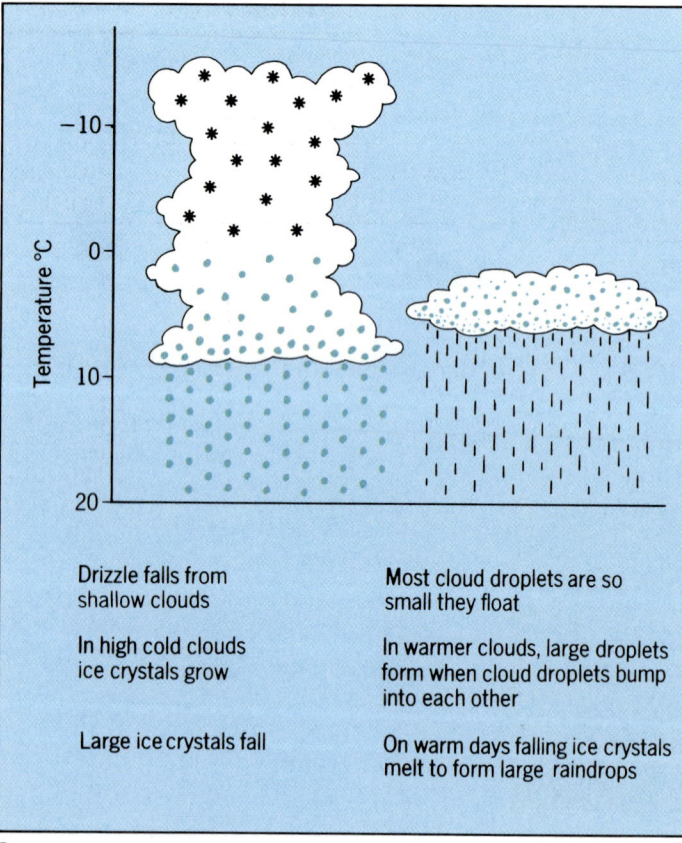

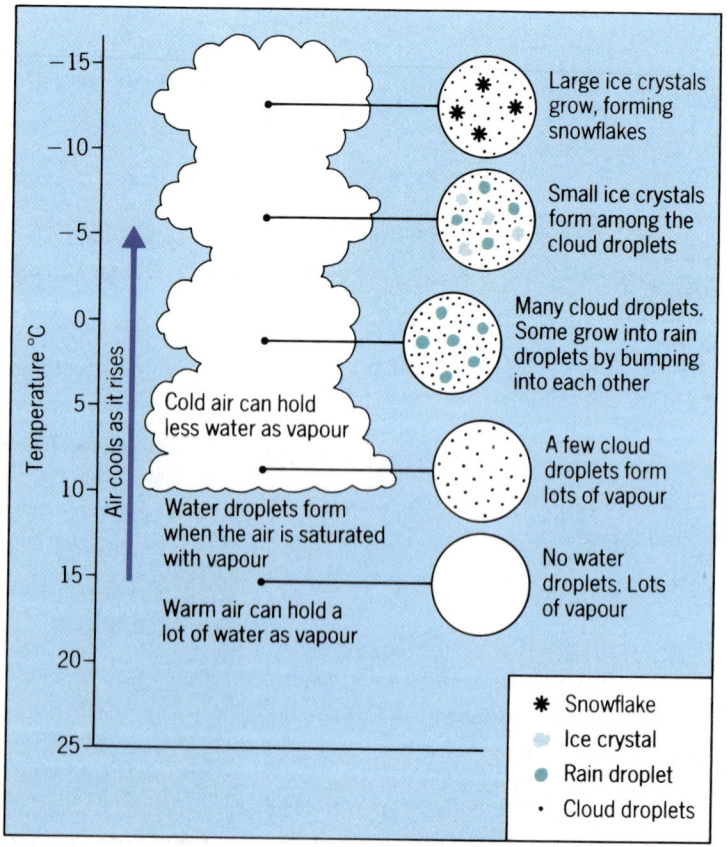

A Relief

- Over 500 m
- 150–500 m
- Below 150 m

B Rainfall

- Over 1500 mm
- 750–1500 mm
- Below 750 mm

C Clouds and rainfall

Drizzle falls from shallow clouds

In high cold clouds ice crystals grow

Large ice crystals fall

Most cloud droplets are so small they float

In warmer clouds, large droplets form when cloud droplets bump into each other

On warm days falling ice crystals melt to form large raindrops

D How rain droplets and snowflakes form as air rises

- Large ice crystals grow, forming snowflakes
- Small ice crystals form among the cloud droplets
- Many cloud droplets. Some grow into rain droplets by bumping into each other
- A few cloud droplets form lots of vapour
- No water droplets. Lots of vapour

Cold air can hold less water as vapour

Water droplets form when the air is saturated with vapour

Warm air can hold a lot of water as vapour

Air cools as it rises

- ✱ Snowflake
- Ice crystal
- Rain droplet
- · Cloud droplets

22

E Relief rainfall

F Convection

On a sunny day if the ground becomes hot, it will heat the air above it which will rise by **convection** (F). This rising air may form shower **clouds**.

Most rain in the British Isles occurs when warm and cold air masses meet along **fronts** (H). The warm air is forced to rise over the cold air which often results in rain (I).

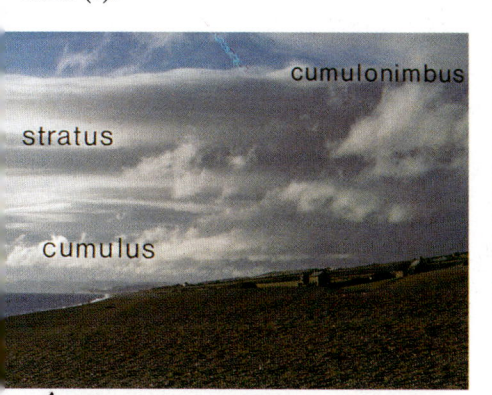

G Cold front weather

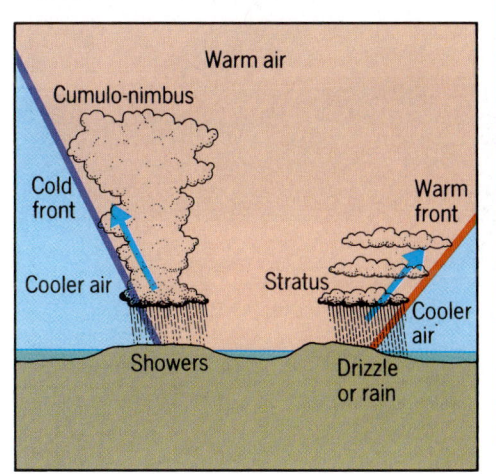

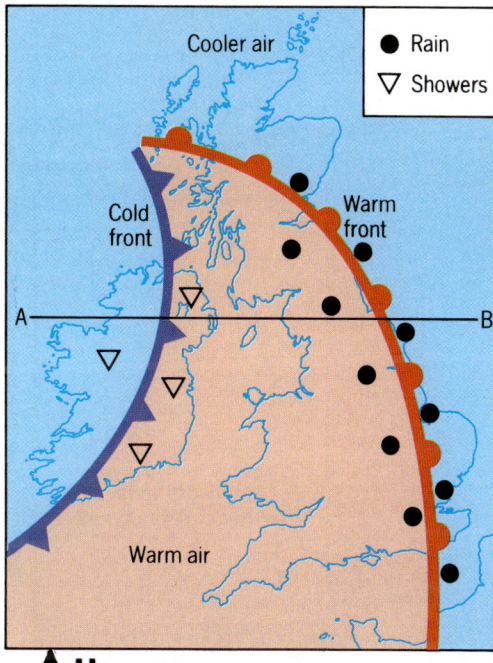

H Frontal rain over Britain

I Cross section A–B

J Warm front weather

1. Look at map B. Which parts of Britain (north, south, east or west) are wettest? Which are driest?

2. Make tracings of maps A and B. Use your atlas to add place-names to your maps. Shade the wettest and highest areas in different colours. What do you notice?

3. Copy C and put the labels in the right places. Use D to help you.

4. Using information from D explain why there is cloud and rain over the mountains in photo E.

5. Copy the table below and fill in the spaces using the information on these pages.

Type of rainfall		Why the air rises	Type of rain	Type of cloud
Relief		Forced over mountains		
Convection				Cumulo-nimbus
F R O N T A L	Warm front			
	Cold front		Heavy showers	

Gg 1/5b; Gg 3/5a, 6a, 6c 23

Winding it up

Winds are caused by differences in air **pressure**. Wind is air moving from *high* pressure to *low* pressure. The greater the pressure difference the stronger the wind (A–D).

INDIA HIT BY 300 kmh WINDS

Cyclone GAY became one of the most powerful storms of this year as it approached India this week. Maximum wind speeds were estimated to be about 300 kmh.

37 DEAD IN GALE HAVOC

Devastation as *170 kmh* winds smash Britain.

A Newspaper reports ▷

Symbol	Wind speed (knots)
◎	Calm
	1–2
	3–7
	8–12
	13–17
For each additional half-feather add five knots	
	48–52
	52–57

▲ C

B Surface weather chart for 1200 GMT on 25 January 1990 (Drawn using information supplied by the Meteorological Office)

D

24

I *The Beaufort wind-scale. This is used as a simple way of estimating wind speed when there is no anemometer available (see page 16)*

Force number	Speed in kmh	Description	What happens
0	0–1	Calm	Smoke goes straight up.
1	2–5	Light air	Smoke drifts but wind-vane does not turn.
2	6–11	Light breeze	Leaves rustle. Wind felt on face. Wind-vane moves.
3	12–19	Gentle breeze	Leaves and twigs move all the time. Flags flutter.
4	20–28	Moderate breeze	Small branches move. Dust raised. Paper blows about.
5	29–38	Fresh breeze	Small trees begin to sway.
6	39–49	Strong breeze	Large branches move. Telegraph wires whistle. Umbrella difficult to hold.
7	50–61	Near gale	Whole trees move. Hard to walk against the wind.
8	62–74	Gale	Twigs and branches broken from trees.
9	75–87	Strong Gale	Damage occurs. Chimney pots and slates blown off.
10	88–102	Storm	Trees uprooted. Seldom happens in the British Isles.

△ **E**

△ **F**

△ **G**

H *Pumping up a bicycle tyre and blowing up a balloon*

1 Look at map B.
   a What is the highest wind speed marked?
   b What is the lowest wind speed marked?
   c In which directions were the strongest winds blowing?
   d Over which part of Britain was the area of lowest pressure?

2 Describe the damage shown in photographs C and D. Page 11 gives more information about the winds on this day.

3 What wind speed on the Beaufort wind-scale (I) do E, F and G illustrate?

4 Draw pictures to illustrate wind speeds 3, 6 and 9 on the Beaufort wind-scale.

5 Look outside. What is the wind speed and direction today?

6 **a** What happens when we blow up a balloon and let it go without tying it up (H)?
   b What happens when a tyre gets a puncture (H)?

Investigating water movements

Water movements depend on where the water falls and how heavy the rainfall is. Water will: be **intercepted** (not reach the ground), **infiltrate** (sink into the ground) or **runoff** (flow away over the ground). These are shown in A.

Interception varies with the type and number of trees and the time of year (C and D).
Infiltration depends on the surface the water falls on.
Permeable surfaces, like chalk rock or sand (D) allow water to sink in.
Impermeable surfaces, like clay or tarmac (B), prevent water from sinking in.

Water which does not sink in becomes runoff. Steep slopes and impermeable surfaces will have large amounts of runoff.

A *Interception, infiltration and runoff*

B *School playground*

C *Woodland in winter (frozen ground)*

D *Woodland in summer (sandy soil)*

Photo letter ...	1 ... 5	
All rain intercepted		No rain intercepted
Fast infiltration		No infiltration
High runoff		No runoff

1. For each location in diagram A, (1, 2, 3 or 4) decide whether water would infiltrate into the ground quickly or slowly. Give reasons for your decisions.

2. Draw a labelled copy of A showing the different water movements that could occur if it rains.

3. Draw a sketch of photo D. Label where interception, infiltration and runoff will occur if it rains.

4. Study photographs B, C and D. Copy and complete the table on the left three times, once for each photo. Fill in the middle column on each with a number between 1 and 5. One is the top score for amounts of interception, infiltration and runoff. Five means there is none.

Water movements in rivers

Most water that falls to the ground will end up in a river. By observing and measuring water-flows in rivers people can predict and prevent flooding.

The students in H wanted to measure the water-flow in a small stream.

They chose a short stretch of stream and drew a sketch-map (G). They dropped an orange into the stream at point A, observed its path down the stream and recorded it on their sketch-map.

They also measured the speed of the water in the stream. Helen dropped the orange in at point A five times and Darren collected it at point B. Javed measured and recorded the time it took to travel between A and B (E).

It rained on the day they did their study so they were also able to measure the rainfall and the changes in the water-level of the stream. Graph F shows their results.

F *A hydrograph for Millbrook Stream*

Shallow water, orange would move quickly

Deeper water, orange moved slowly

G *Sketch-map to show water-flow in a stream*

H *Measuring river velocity*

E Water velocity record sheet

Distance: 10 metres   Date: 23/11/90
Location: MILLBROOK   Time: 14.25

Observation	Time (secs)
1	28
2	31
3	32
4	28
5	31
Total	
Average	

Velocity = $\dfrac{\text{Distance}}{\text{Average time}}$ = metres/sec

---

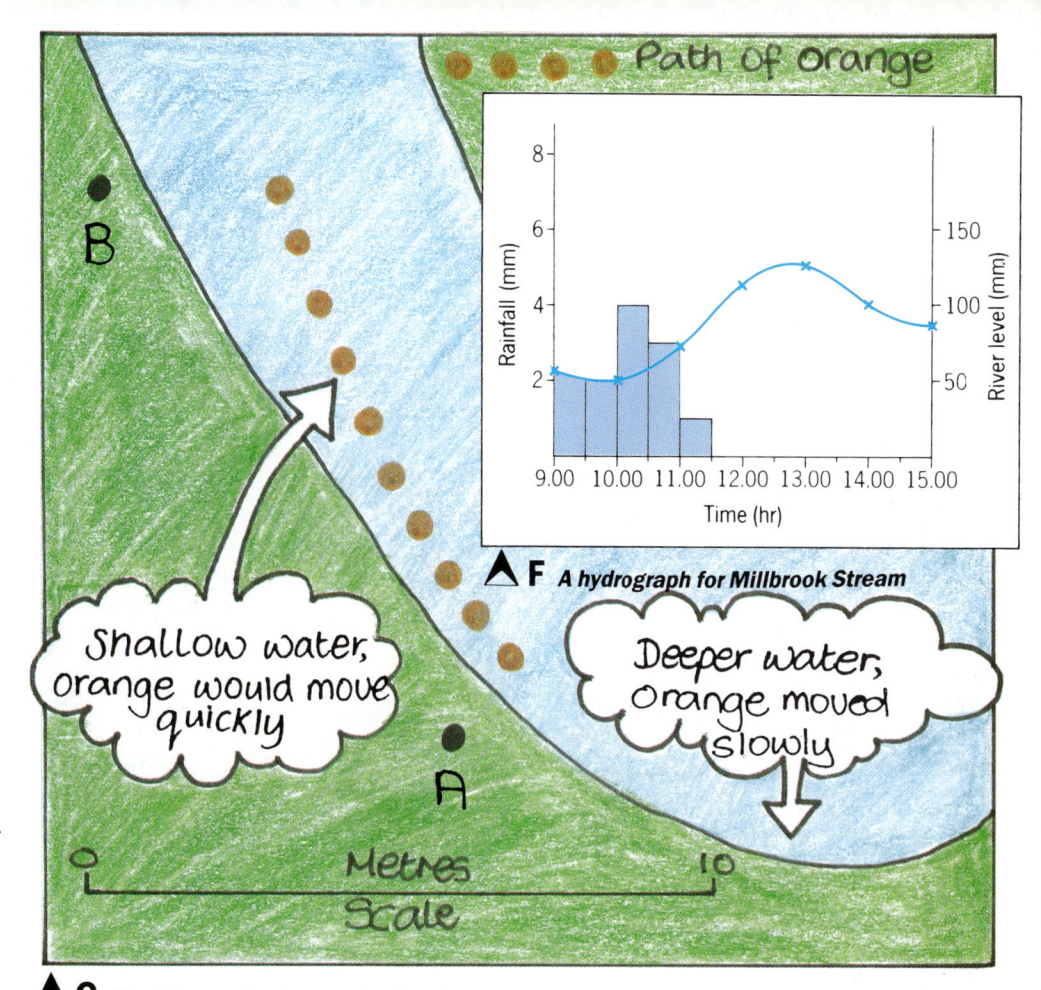

5 Study map G.
 a Describe the path of the orange down the stream.
 b What happens to the speed of the orange as the water gets shallower or deeper?

6 Use the information on record sheet E.
 a Work out the average time taken for the orange to travel between A and B.
 b Work out the average speed (velocity) of the stream.

7 a Describe what happened to the water-level in the stream during and after the rain (F).
 b How could this information be used to predict flooding?

Processes in river channels

A working river

Water flowing in a river channel works hard. It **erodes** (wears away), **transports** (carries) and **deposits** (drops) material (C and D). The power of a river to do this work depends on the speed of the water-flow (A and B). Rivers do most work when they are in flood (C). **Deposition** occurs at any part of the river when water is slowed and the river has to drop some material

▲ **A** Slow flow in a river channel

▲ **B** Fast flow down a gully

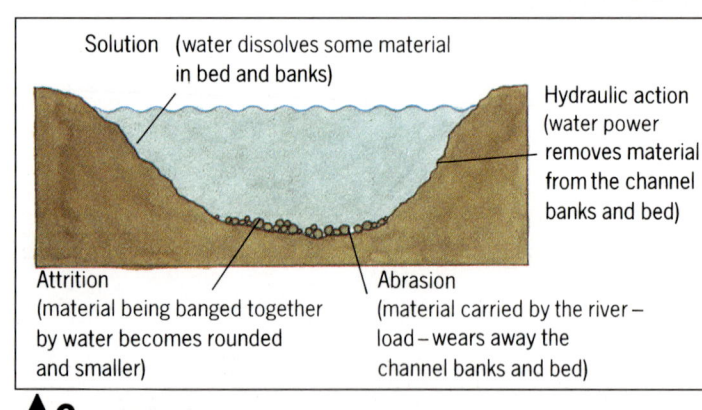

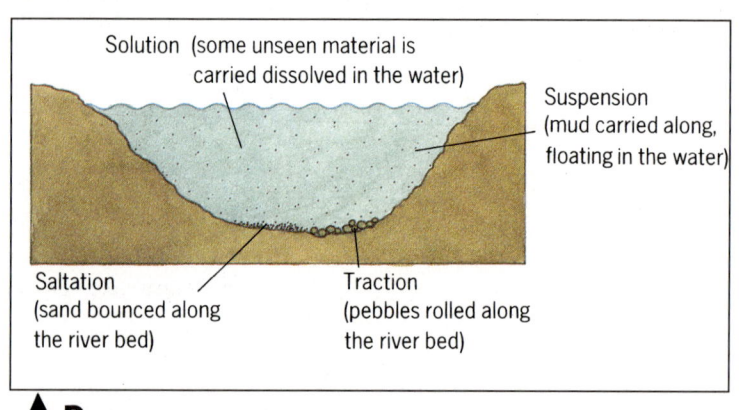

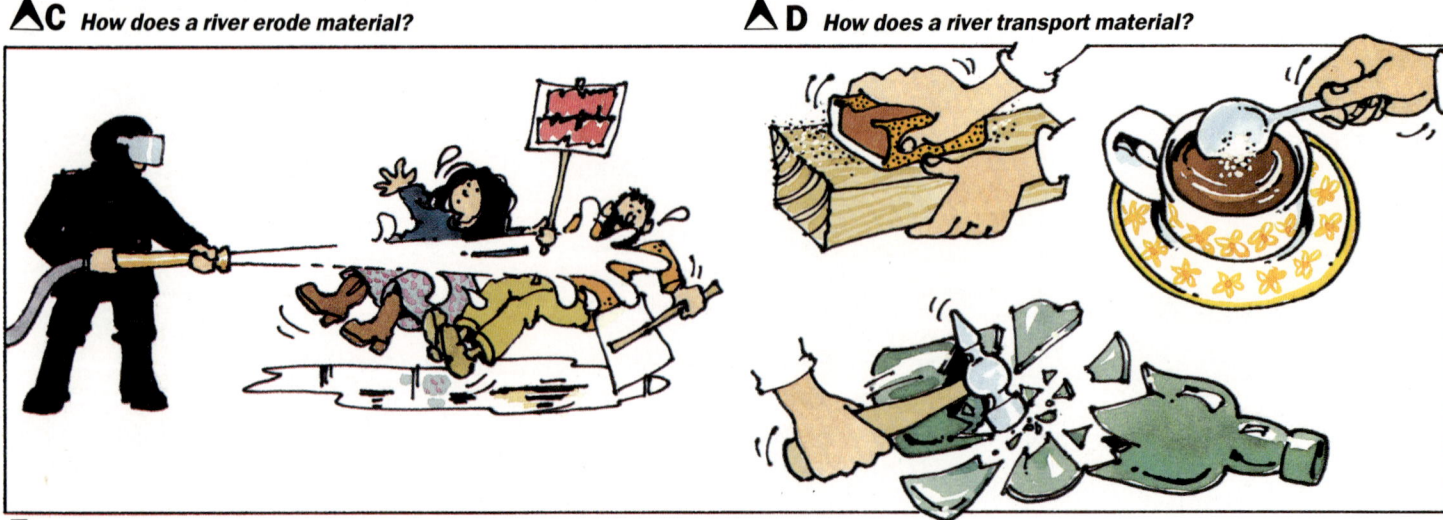

Solution (water dissolves some material in bed and banks)

Hydraulic action (water power removes material from the channel banks and bed)

Attrition (material being banged together by water becomes rounded and smaller)

Abrasion (material carried by the river – load – wears away the channel banks and bed)

▲ **C** How does a river erode material?

Solution (some unseen material is carried dissolved in the water)

Suspension (mud carried along, floating in the water)

Saltation (sand bounced along the river bed)

Traction (pebbles rolled along the river bed)

▲ **D** How does a river transport material?

E Eroding rivers are like . . .

28

Meanders (G) are bends in the river. Fast-flowing water on the outside of the bend erodes the bank while the slow-flowing water on the inside deposits material (F).

Waterfalls (H and I) are formed when the river has difficulty eroding a band of hard rock.

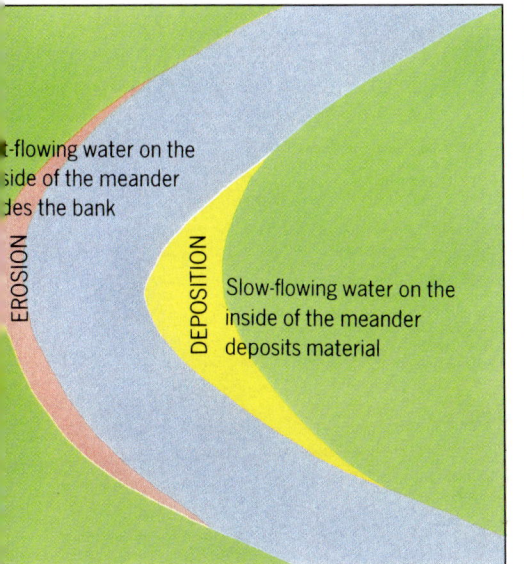

F *Erosion and deposition on a meander (river bend)*

Fast-flowing water on the outside of the meander erodes the bank

EROSION

DEPOSITION

Slow-flowing water on the inside of the meander deposits material

▲ **G** *A river meander*

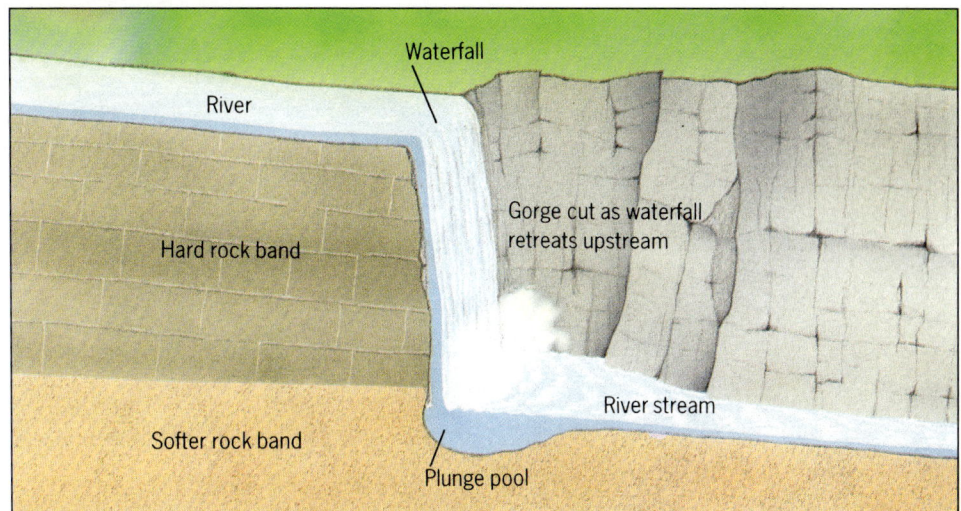

H *How a waterfall forms*

River — Waterfall — Hard rock band — Gorge cut as waterfall retreats upstream — Softer rock band — Plunge pool — River stream

I *A waterfall in Guadeloupe*

1. What evidence is there in photos A and B of the power of rivers to erode, transport and deposit material? Use the terms in C and D in your answer.

2. Match the drawings in E with the labels about river erosion in C.

3. 'Rivers do most work when they flow fast or flood.' In pairs discuss the evidence for this statement. You may need to refer back to page 13.

4. **a** Draw a sketch of G to show the erosion on the outside of the bend and deposition on the inside.
   b Over time, what will happen to the grass on the outside of the bend in G?
   c If houses were built on the river banks, how could they be protected from erosion?

5. **a** Why are deep pools (**plunge pools**) formed at the foot of waterfalls?
   b How is the plunge pool in I being used?

Gg 3/4b, 5c, 6e

River valley landforms

Each river valley is different but there are *three* commonly found shapes (A, B and C).

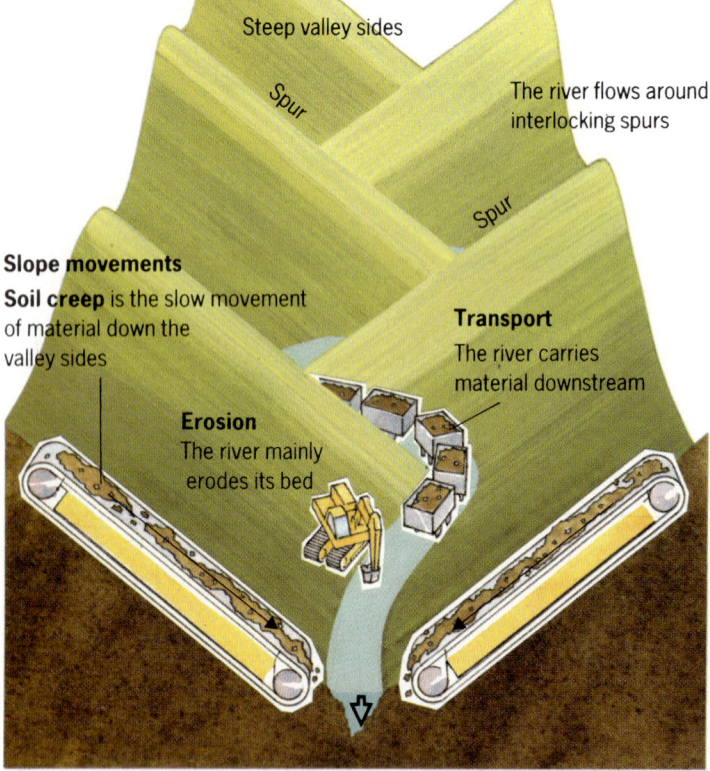

The river eroding downwards forms a narrow steep-sided valley

Steep valley sides

Spur

The river flows around interlocking spurs

Spur

Slope movements
Soil creep is the slow movement of material down the valley sides

Transport
The river carries material downstream

Erosion
The river mainly erodes its bed

▲ **A** *A river eroding downwards*

The river eroding sideways forms a flat-floored valley with straight sides

River bluffs

Erosion
The river erodes its bank and the valley sides by meandering

Transport

Deposition
Material is dumped on the floodplain when the river floods

Slope movements

Sediments

Rock

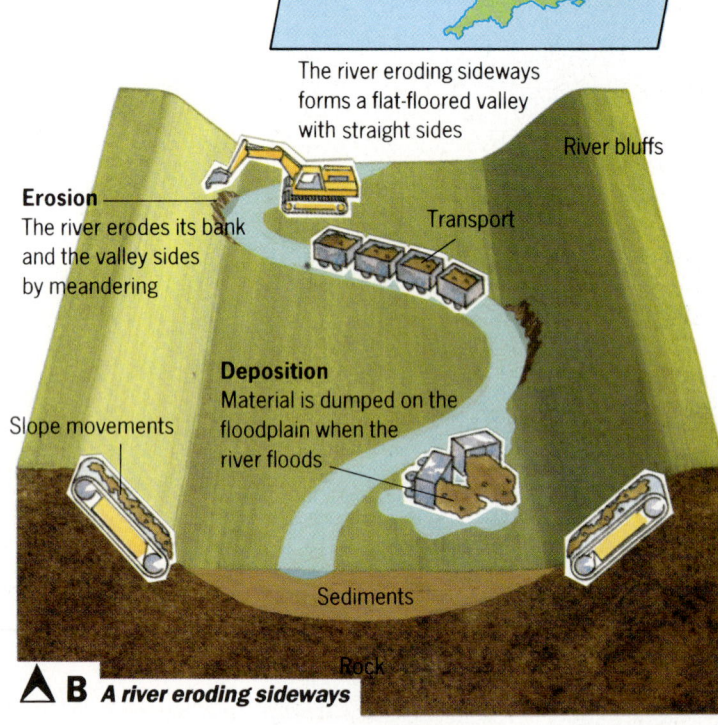

▲ **B** *A river eroding sideways*

River Wye

C *A river depositing material*

The river depositing material forms a wide valley with gentle slopes

Flat or gently sloping valley floor

Gentle valley sides

Transport

Floodplain

Slope movements are very slow because the slopes are gentle

Deposition
Floods are common

Sediment

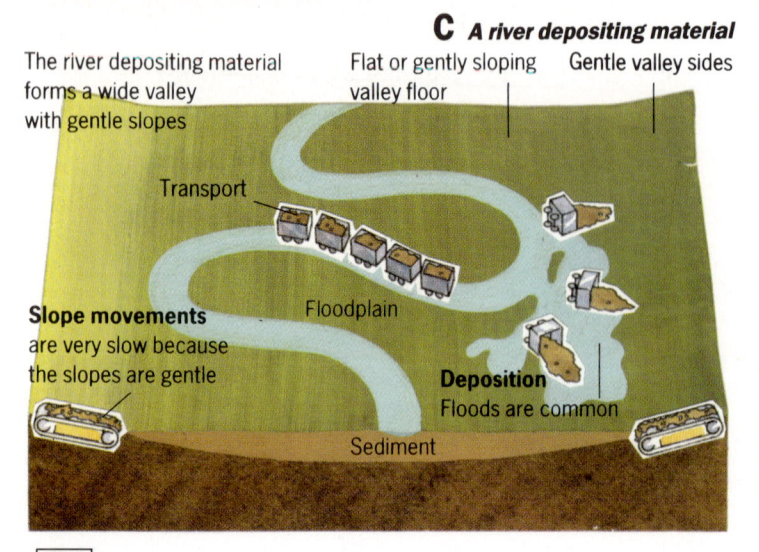

Flow	A person digging	A train of trucks	A train of trucks
NORMAL	with a spade	empty	running smoothly
FLOOD	with a JCB	full	derailed
Process	Erosion	Transport	Deposition

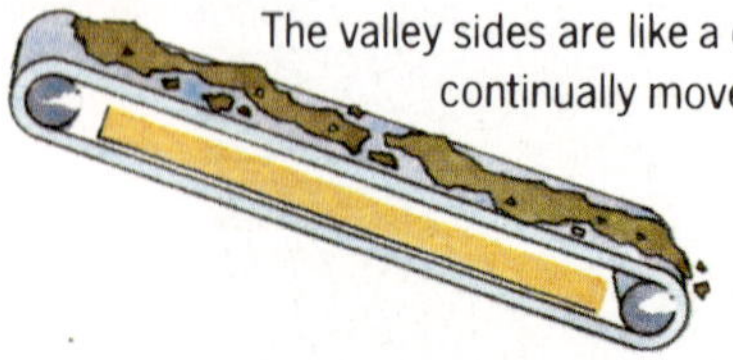

The valley sides are like a conveyor belt which continually moves material downhill

D *The processes of river valley formation*

30

The valley of the River Wye

The River Wye flows from its **source** on Plynlimon in mid Wales to its **mouth** near Chepstow on the Severn Estuary.

E The Wye Valley near its source on Plynlimon

F The Elan Valley and Reservoir

G View of Tintern Abbey from Devil's Pulpit

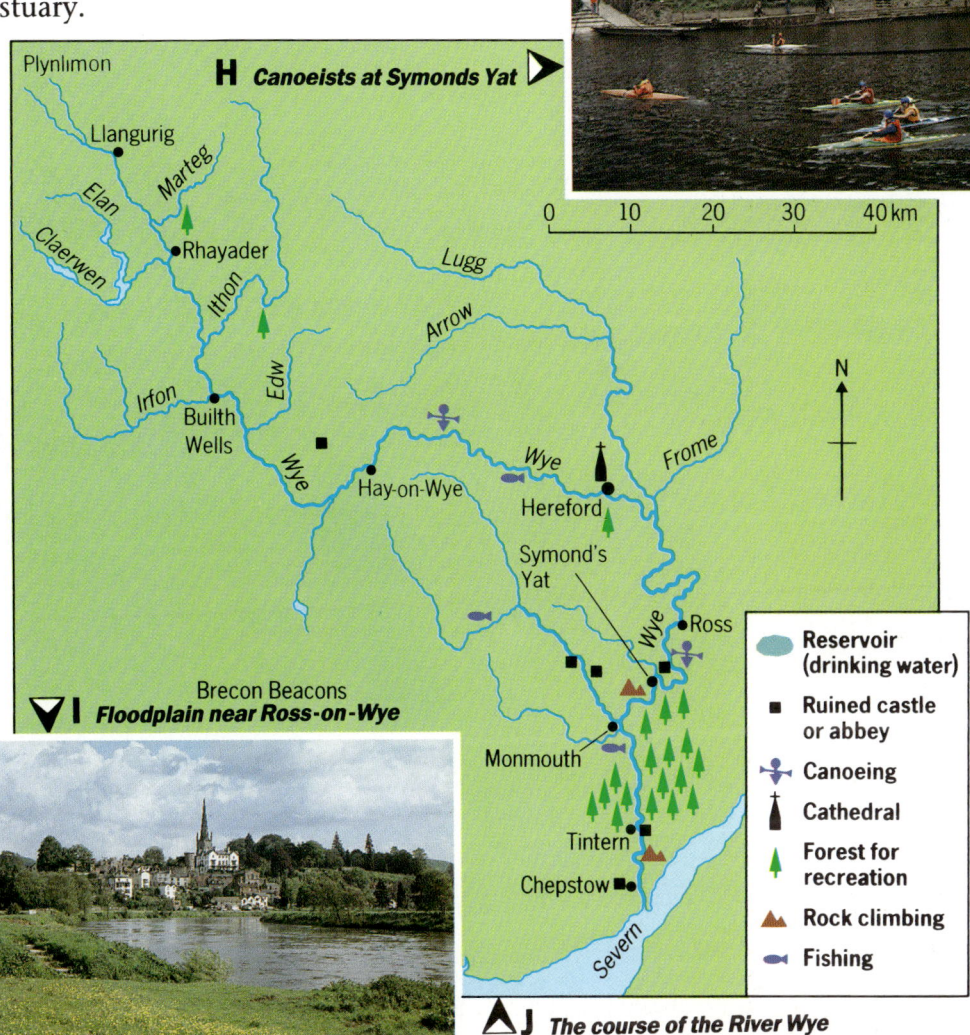

H Canoeists at Symonds Yat

I Floodplain near Ross-on-Wye

J The course of the River Wye

Key:
- Reservoir (drinking water)
- Ruined castle or abbey
- Canoeing
- Cathedral
- Forest for recreation
- Rock climbing
- Fishing

1. Using information from A–D, describe the different processes involved in making a valley.

2. **a** Make two sketches of the valley shapes in photographs E and I.
   b Add labels from the list below to your sketches. You will not need all the labels for each sketch.
   - Flood plain
   - Steep valley side
   - River bluff
   - Spur
   c Explain the processes that have formed these two valleys.

3. The Wye valley is a popular tourist area because of its beautiful river valley. Using evidence from these pages, produce a leaflet for tourists that introduces them to the area. You should include:
   - a map
   - what the scenery looks like
   - leisure activities
   - towns and historic places to visit.

Gg 3/4b, 4c, 5c, 6e

River basins

A The Yangtze River basin

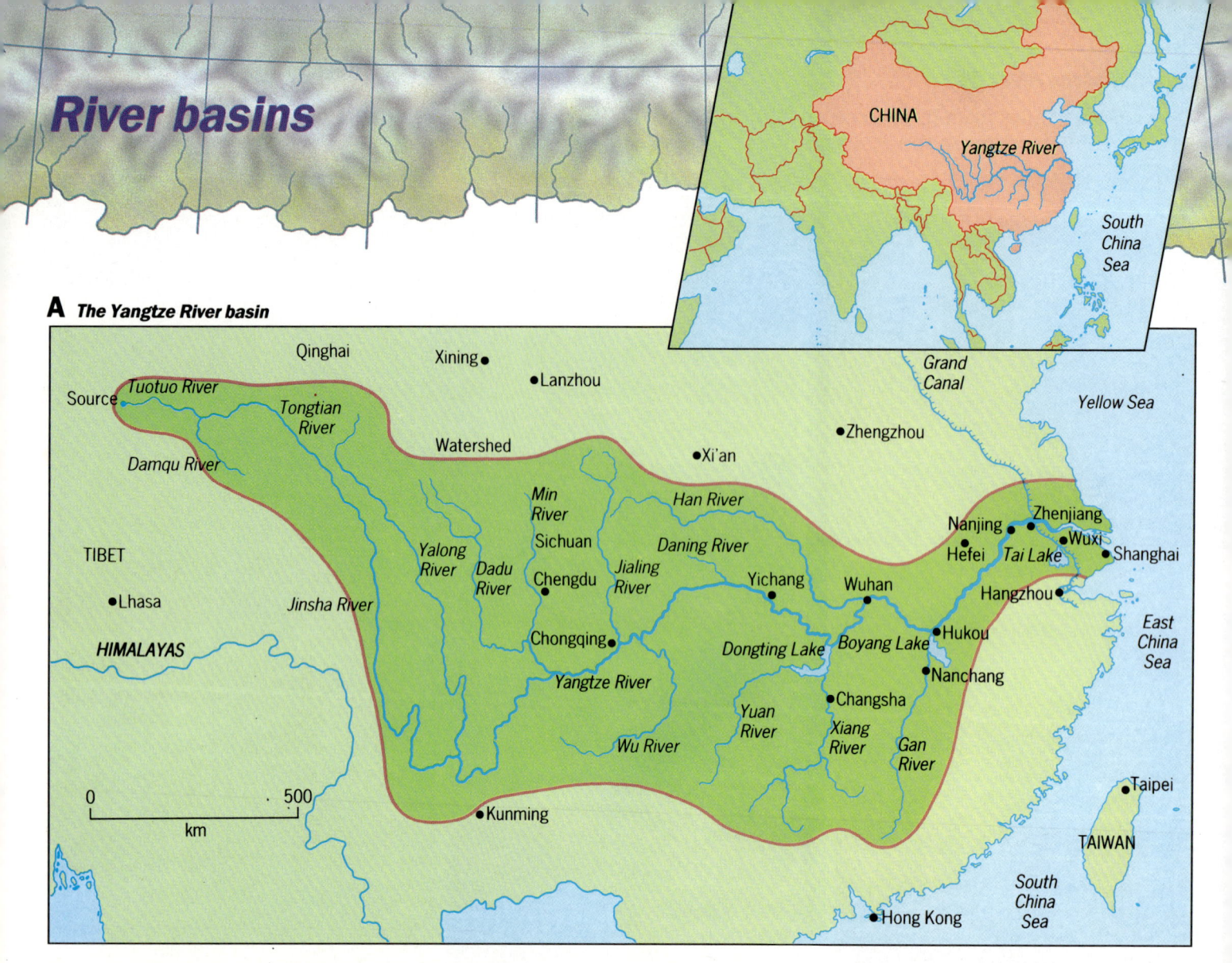

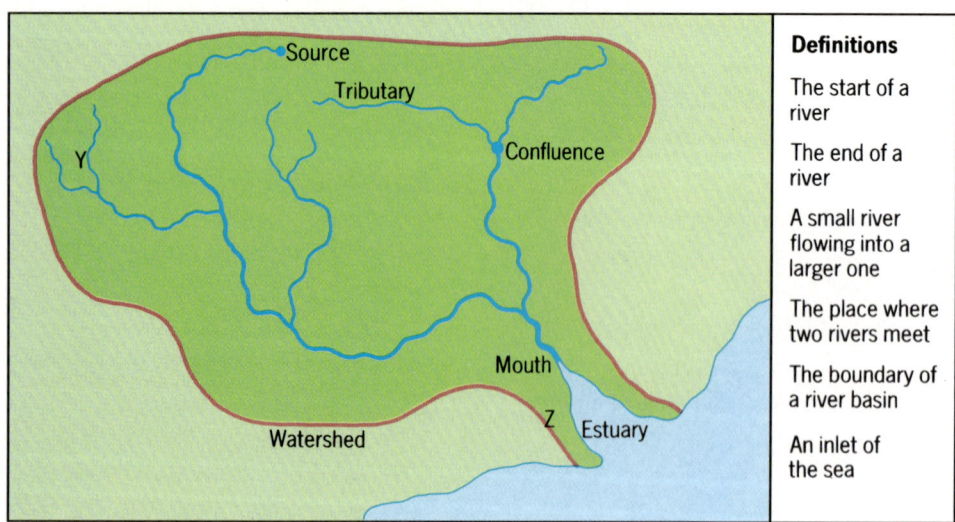

Definitions	
Source	The start of a river
Mouth	The end of a river
Tributary	A small river flowing into a larger one
Confluence	The place where two rivers meet
Watershed	The boundary of a river basin
Estuary	An inlet of the sea

B A river basin

Much of the water falling to the ground eventually finds its way into a river and then into the sea. The area that a river collects its water from is called its **drainage basin** or **catchment area** (B).

The Yangtze River basin

The Yangtze River (A), in China, has the third largest river basin in the world. The landscape and scenery change as the river flows from its source to its mouth (C–F).

C The upper reaches of the Yangtze

D The middle reaches of the Yangtze

E A rice paddy at the lower reaches of the Yangtze

F The mouth of the Yangtze

1. Match up the terms shown in B with the definitions, e.g:
   Source: the start of a river.

2. Write the story of how a droplet of water falling at Y travels to the sea at Z. Use all the terms in B within your story.

3. Use information from map A to answer these questions about the Yangtze River.
   a Where is its source?
   b Name eight tributaries.
   c How far is it between Hukou and Nanjing?
   d Name two towns that are sited at **confluences**.
   e Which city is at the **mouth** of the river?

4. Describe the different landscapes and scenery in the river basin. Use the information given in map A and photographs C–F.

Gg 3/4c, 6d 33

Weather differences in the British Isles

A The weather may vary from place to place

Picture white, secluded beaches that stretch for miles at a time. Crystal clear waters that sparkle with fish. A sun that sometimes lights the land for 23 hours of the day. Picture yourself in Scotland.

The Mild Mild West... All Year Round Falmouth CORNWALL
For brochure tel or write (0326) 318618 Dept. V P.O. Box 10, Falmouth, Cornwall

It's so near — and sunshine's here. Only 1 hour 25 mins from London
CLACTON FRINTON-ON-SEA WALTON-ON-THE-NAZE ST OSYTH HARWICH & DOVERCOURT BRIGHTLINGSEA
& FREE Brochure from Room 21 Tourist Info Centre PO Box 552 CLACTON-ON-SEA, Essex CO16 9AQ
24 HOUR PHONE 0255 256155

The **weather** of the British Isles is very varied. It depends on where we live (A and B) and on the time of the year (B and C). It is also affected by the type of **air mass** over the country. There are five main types. They come from different places and bring us a variety of weather conditions (D and E).

B A joke... or is it?

WINTER IN THE LAKE DISTRICT | SUMMER IN THE LAKE DISTRICT

C The weather changes during the year

1989/90	January (Average daily figures)			July (Average daily figures)		
	Sunshine hours	Rainfall (mm)	Max. temp. °C	Sunshine hours	Rainfall (mm)	Max. temp. °C
1 Arisaig	0.8	5.8	9	9.7	1.9	21
2 Aviemore	0.7	6.2	5	6.6	1.5	20
3 Bangor	1.6	2.4	9	8.8	1.8	21
4 Belfast	1.0	3.0	8	8.5	3.0	22
5 Buxton	1.3	4.8	7	8.2	3.2	22
6 Clacton	2.0	1.5	8	8.9	1.0	22
7 Falmouth	1.3	4.2	11	9.2	2.3	24
8 Keswick	0.8	5.5	8	9.7	3.9	23
9 Limerick	1.0	3.0	5	8.6	2.5	19
10 London	1.8	1.7	9	9.3	1.8	26
11 Ross-on-Wye	1.5	2.4	10	9.5	1.7	26

D *Air masses and where they come from*

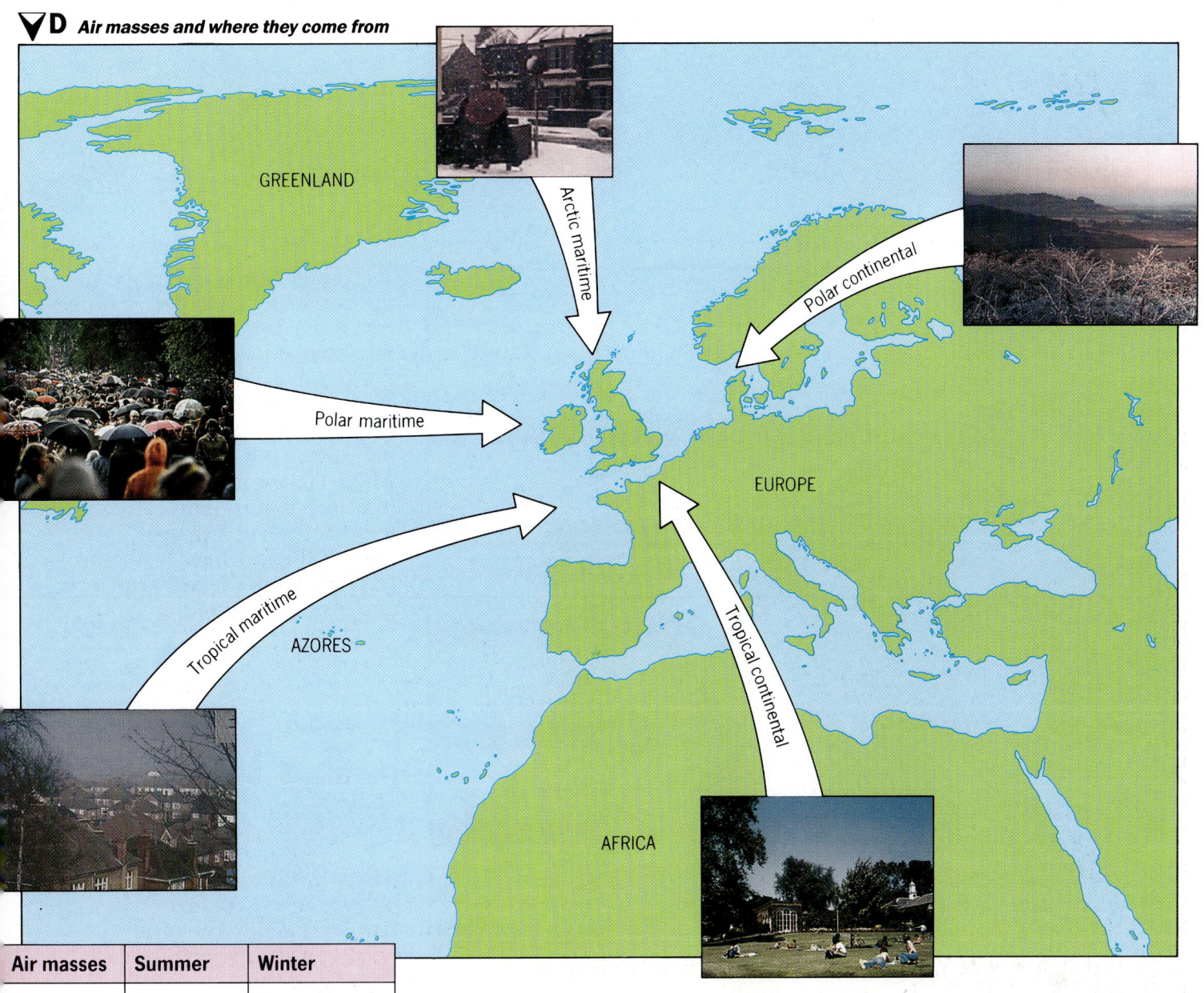

Air masses	Summer	Winter
Arctic maritime	Rare	Very cold winds Snow
Polar maritime (very common)	Wet Cool	Strong winds Cold Showers (sometimes snow)
Polar continental	Heatwaves	Cold winds Relatively dry Frost
Tropical maritime (very common)	Moist Relatively cool	Mild Mist/fog
Tropical continental	Hot Dry Sunny	Does not occur

1   **a** Look at A. Write down what is said about the weather for each of the three places.
    b Using the information in C say whether you think the adverts give a true picture about each place.

2   Is B a joke or not? Check it out using C.

3   From C find the place which is:
    a the warmest
    b the sunniest
    c the wettest.

4   For each of the pictures in D
    a describe the weather conditions;
    b say whether you think it is summer or winter.

5   Consider where the air masses come from. Say which you think would bring the types of weather in the list:
    a coldest
    b warmest
    c wettest.

Gg 3/5a, 5b, 6b   35

Latitude, land and sea

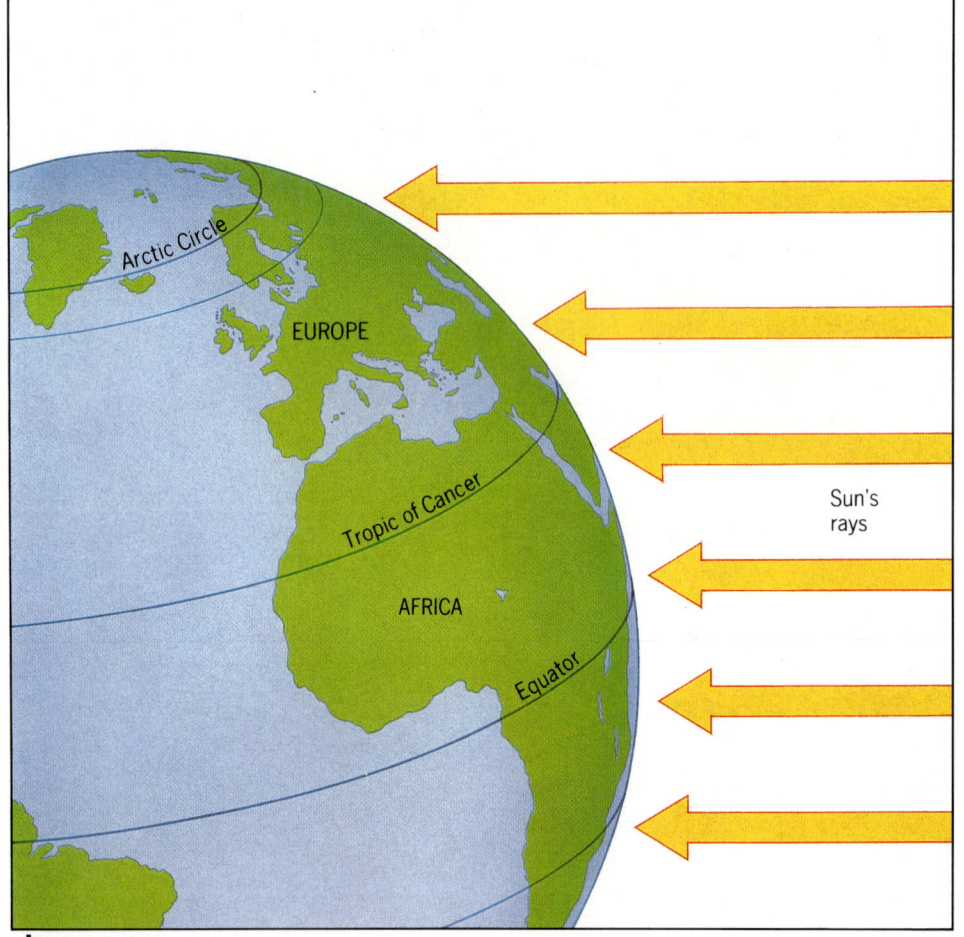

The temperatures in Europe are influenced by **latitude**, in other words the distance from the **Equator** (A).

The sun's rays hit the earth in straight lines. B shows that because the earth's surface is curved, the rays spread out more at X (about where Europe is) than they do at Y (on the Equator). This causes lower temperatures at X than at Y. Also, to reach X the rays have further to travel through the **atmosphere** and heat is lost there.

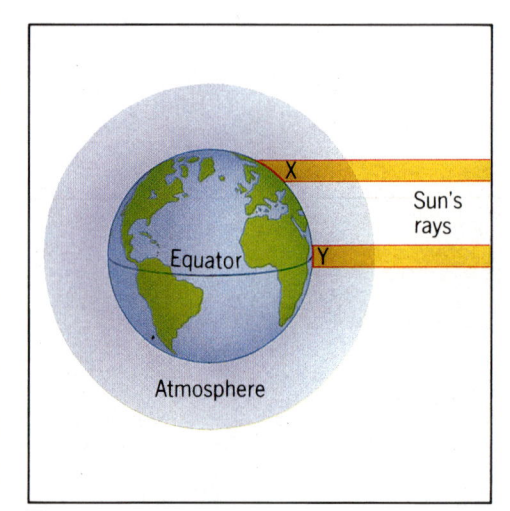

A The latitude

B Angles of the sun's rays

C Moscow in winter

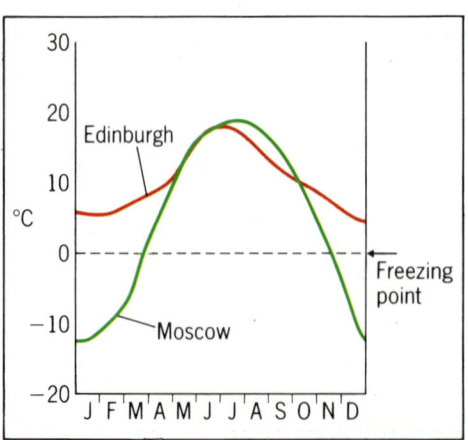

D Temperatures in Moscow and Edinburgh

E Average sea temperatures around Britain

Month	°C	Month	°C
January	8	July	13
February	6	August	14
March	6	September	15
April	8	October	14
May	10	November	12
June	12	December	10

Latitude is not the only factor to affect temperatures. Although Moscow and Edinburgh are on the same latitude their **climates** are different (C and D). Why? (The clue is the sea.)

During the year the sea heats up slowly in the summer and cools down slowly in the winter (E). The land does the opposite. Being close to the sea helps to keep temperatures up (F). In particular a warm ocean current called the **North Atlantic Drift** prevents British temperatures from dropping too low (G).

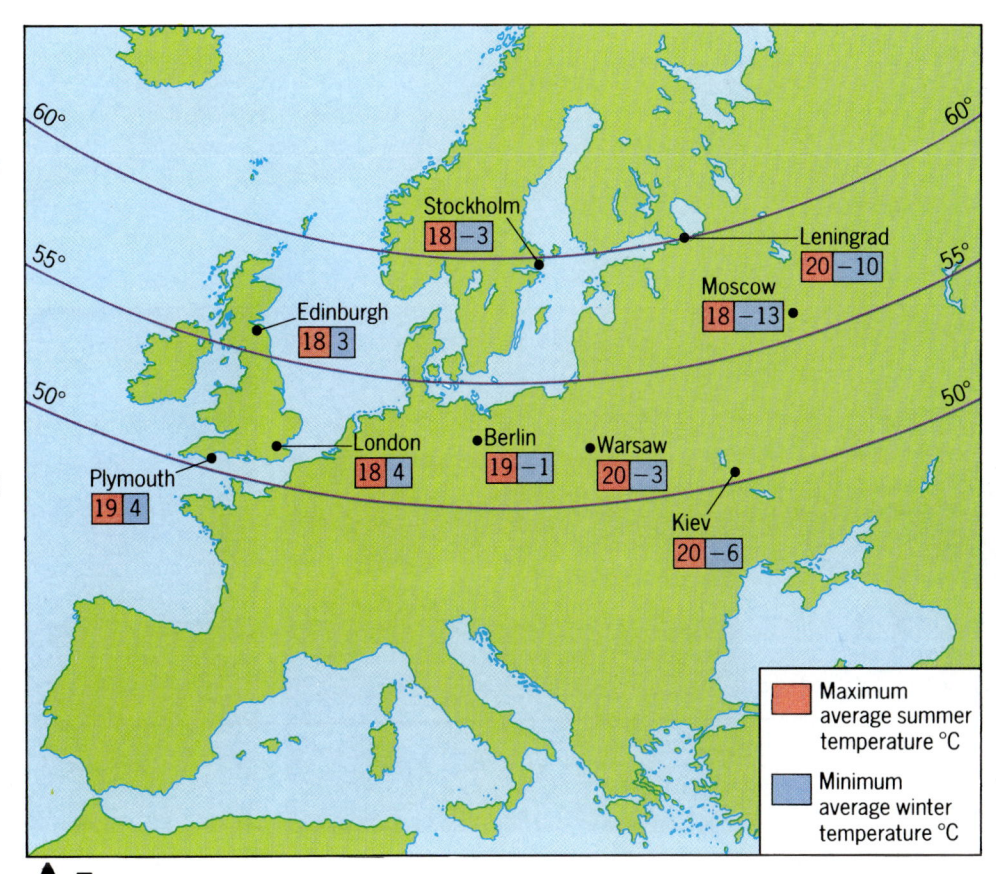

F *The effect of sea and land on temperatures*

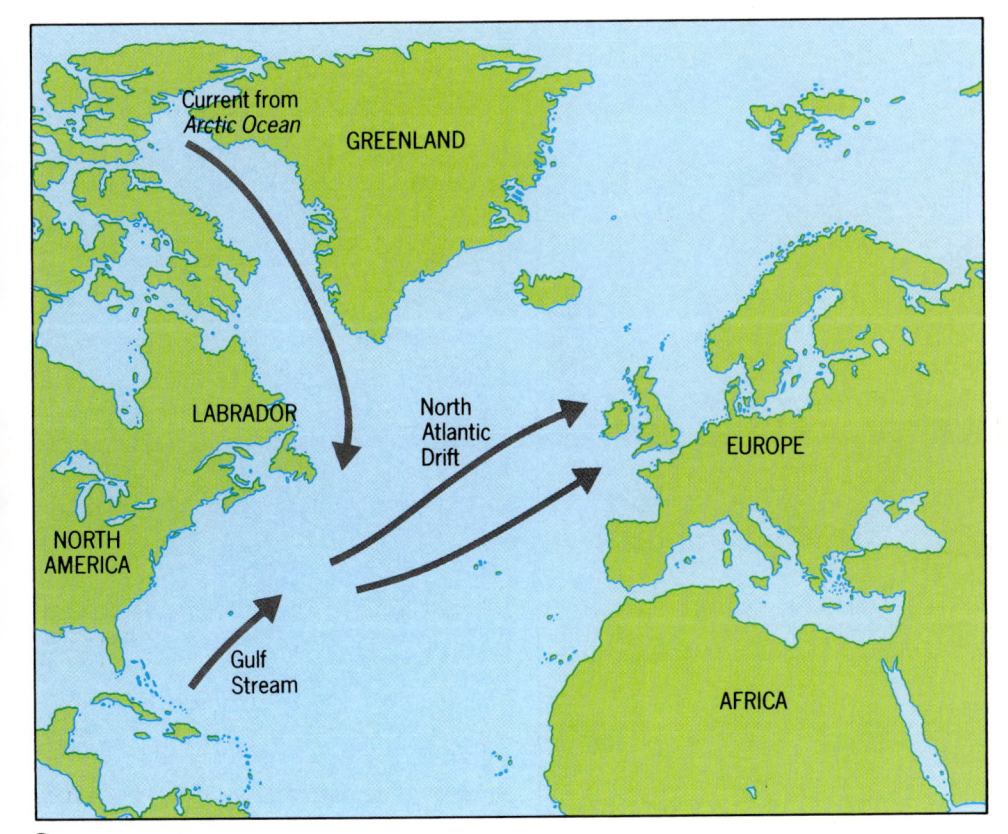

G *Britain benefits from the North Atlantic Drift*

1. On tracing paper draw a graph using the scale from D and the information from E. Lay your graph over D and describe how the sea temperatures compare with:
   a Moscow
   b Edinburgh

2. How would the differences in the weather between Plymouth and Leningrad affect the people who live there? Use the following headings in your answer: clothes, transport, houses and leisure-time activities.

3. Labrador (North America) is on the same latitude as Britain but has a colder climate. Use G to explain why.

The spinning earth

A Seasonal changes: summer and winter . . .

B . . . and spring

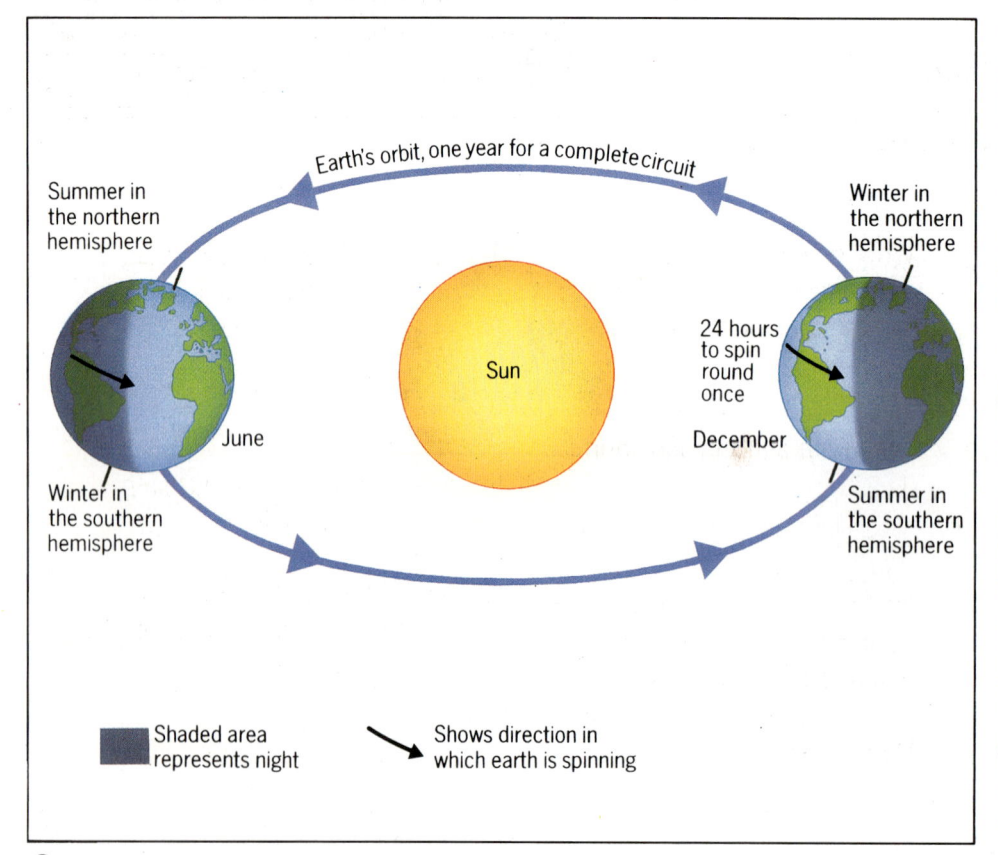

Summer in the northern hemisphere

Earth's orbit, one year for a complete circuit

Winter in the northern hemisphere

Sun

24 hours to spin round once

June

December

Winter in the southern hemisphere

Summer in the southern hemisphere

Shaded area represents night

Shows direction in which earth is spinning

C Positions of the earth during the year

Friday 21st December

I nearly overslept this morning – it's really dark, even at 8 o'clock. Thank goodness it was the last day of term today.

David was told off for opening all the windows in the classroom. Serves him right – it was freezing! As a treat, Dad came to pick us up so we got home in time for the start of Children's TV. It was already getting dark, so it was nice to switch on the fire, pull the curtains and have a hot drink. Only 4 days left until Christmas!

D Dear Diary

E Arctic climates in summer... and winter

F Equatorial climate

Both the **poles** have six months of nearly continuous daylight and six months of nearly continuous darkness. They do not have **seasons** like Britain does (E and G). Nor do the areas around the **equator** (F and H).

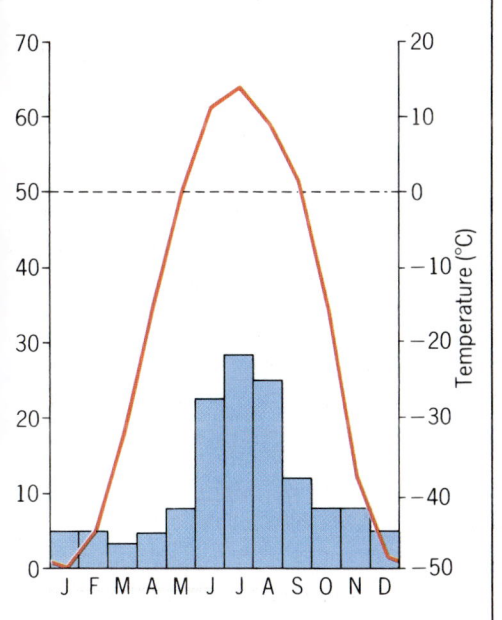

H Climate figures for an equatorial climate

Months	Jan	Feb	Mar	Apr	May	June	July	Aug	Sept	Oct	Nov	Dec
Rainfall (mm)	249	231	262	221	170	84	58	38	46	107	142	203
Temperature (°C)	28	28	28	27	28	28	28	28	29	29	29	28

Manaus, Brazil, located between the Equator and latitude 10 °S

1. Write down three words or phrases about each of the four seasons in Britain. Say which you like best and why.

2. Redraw C showing where you would put autumn and spring (Northern hemisphere).

3. **a** Read D. What does it tell us about winter?
   b What might the person say in their diary on 21 June?
   c Use C to explain the differences between June and December.

4. Photo E shows the two main seasons of the Arctic climate. Use this and G to describe the weather in December and June. Use C to explain the differences.

5. **a** Draw climate graphs using the information in H. Set your graphs out like G.
   b Look at C again. Try to explain why there are no seasons in this area in Brazil.

G Climate graphs for an Arctic climate (Verkhoyansk, USSR)

Gg 3/5a, 6b 39

Hot desert climate

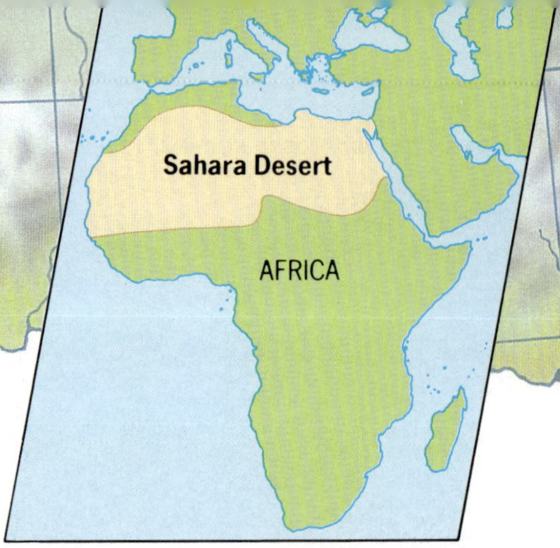

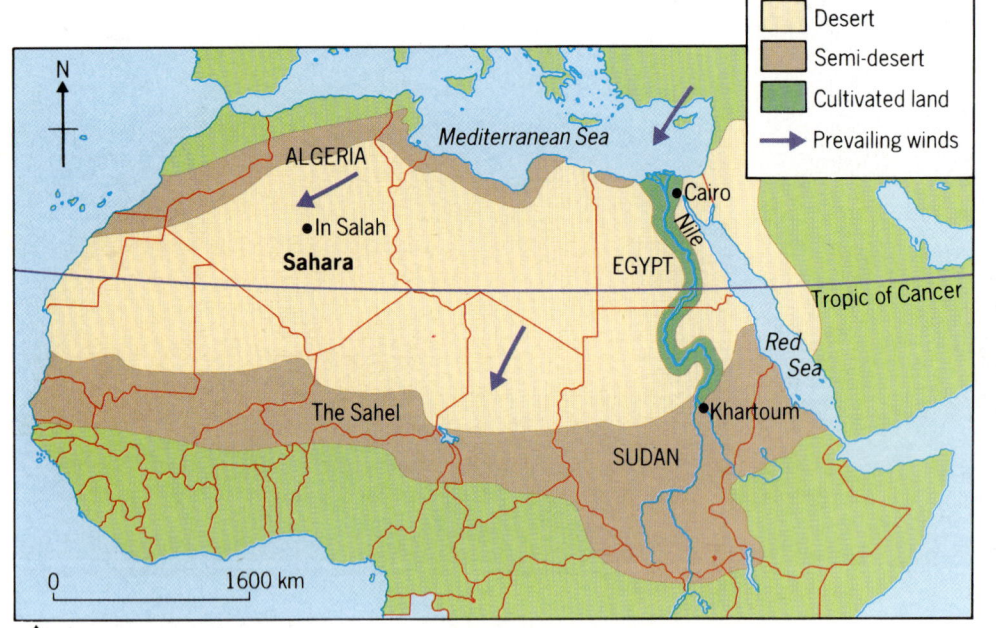

The largest area of **desert** in the world is the Sahara (A). The main winds blowing here are dry, and so only a few **clouds** develop. Rainfall over the year is very low – under 250 mm. Most of this may fall in one or two heavy thunder storms. This sometimes causes **flash floods**.

With a lot of sunshine in the day the bare ground heats up quickly. No cloud at night means that heat is lost very quickly. Temperatures can fall very low, sometimes causing frost.

A The Sahara: location

B Climate figures

		J	F	M	A	M	J	J	A	S	O	N	D
Cairo, Egypt	Rainfall (mm)	5	5	5	3	3	2	0	0	2	2	3	5
	Temperature (°C)	13	15	18	21	25	28	28	28	26	24	20	15
In Salah, Algeria	Rainfall (mm)	2	3	1	1	1	0	0	2	1	1	3	5
	Temperature (°C)	13	16	20	25	29	35	37	36	33	27	19	14

C Day and night in the desert

D The Nile Valley

E Natural vegetation in the desert

Thick waxy leaves to cut down on loss of water. Stems which can store water, e.g. cactus

Roots go deep (up to 15 m) to reach the groundwater, e.g. acacia

Roots spread out just under the surface to make the most of sudden downpours e.g. Creosote bush

F How do plants survive?

G Designed for the desert?

1 **a** Use B to draw two climate graphs.
   b Describe and explain the differences between your graphs of the two places.

2 Most people in Egypt live in the Nile Valley. Look at photos D and E and suggest why.

3 **a** Write down three words or phrases to describe the vegetation in photo E.
   b Use F to help you to explain in your own words how plants can survive in the desert.

4 Copy or trace G. Use these labels on your drawing:
   a Hat to protect head from the sun
   b Fat stored for times when food and water are scarce
   c Broad padded feet for walking easily on sand
   d Long robe to protect skin from the sun
   e Long eyelashes to keep out sand
   f Nostrils which can be closed to keep out sand

Gg 2/3a, 4e, 5a, 6c; Gg 3/6b, 6f

Cold forest climate

IN NORWAY YOU CAN'T FAIL TO ENJOY A FULL DAY.

IT LASTS FOR 24 HOURS.

Remember night-time? It's that dark thing that drops on you like a blanket just when the evening's going so well.

Unless you're in Norway.

In the summer, the sun shines 24 hours a day. You can sit in shirt-sleeves till two in the morning, they have barbeques in the middle of the night. And the further north you venture, the longer the day lasts: in Tromso the sun doesn't set at all for six weeks in midsummer. Even in Oslo, eight hundred miles to the south, it rises at four in the morning and sets after ten thirty at night. And you can ski in the mountains during July; some Norwegian valleys are hotter than Madrid in the summer.

And as half of our country lies within the Arctic Circle we wouldn't deny the existence of some fairly extreme weather conditions.

During several days last summer, for instance, Oslo was the hottest capital city in Europe, with temperatures of over 30 degrees centigrade.

A How about Norway for your summer holidays?

B Some of the things that affect the Scandinavian climate

Most of Scandinavia has a cold forest **climate**. This brings very cold weather in winter and, often, very hot weather in summer. The west coast of Norway is different. It is more like the British climate but cooler. The sea helps keep temperatures higher, and places like Tromso are generally warmer than those on the same **latitude** further inland. The Kiolen Mountains act as a barrier to this warmer climate.

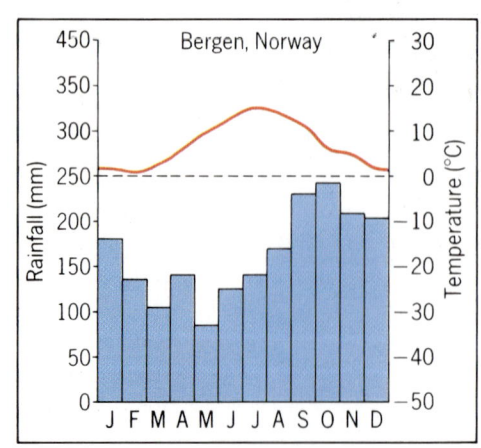

C Climate graphs for Bergen

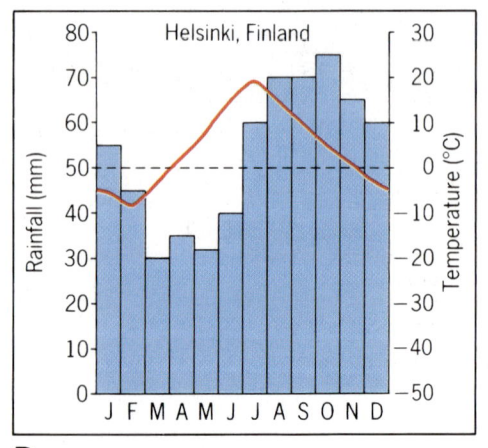

D ...and Helsinki

42

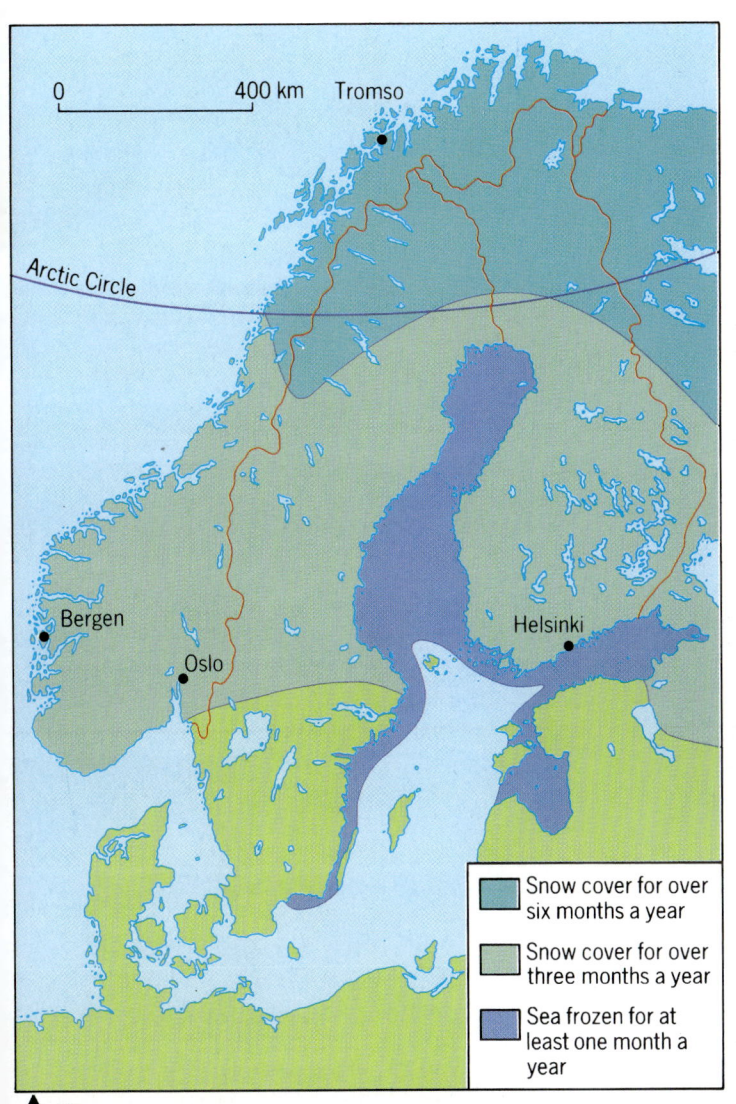

E What to expect in the winter months: snow . . .

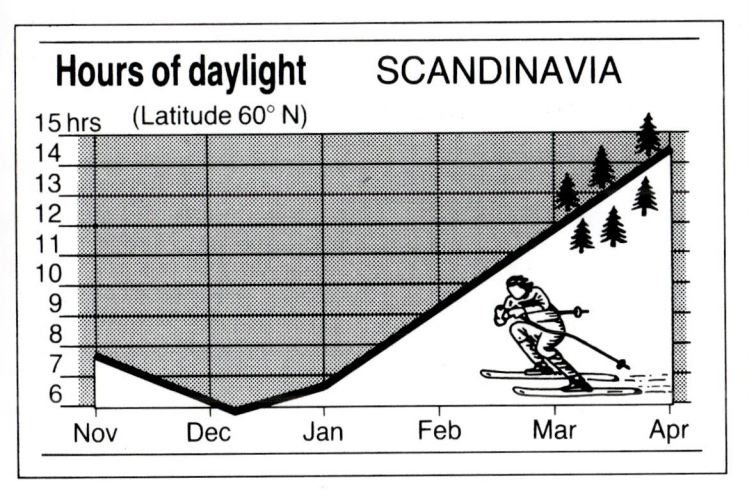

Legend:
- Snow cover for over six months a year
- Snow cover for over three months a year
- Sea frozen for at least one month a year

F . . . and darkness

Hours of daylight — SCANDINAVIA (Latitude 60° N)

G Leisure time – ice sledging

H Leisure time – mountain biking and walking

1 **a** Make a list of the information you are given about the weather and climate in A.
   b Does it give a true picture of Norway's climate? What's missing?

2 **a** Look at C and D and spot the differences between the two places. (Note that the rainfall scales are different).
   b Now look at the climate graph for Verkhoyansk, USSR on page 39. What happens to the climate as you move further north and inland?
   c Study the information on this page. How do the sea and the mountains help explain the differences you saw in questions a and b?

3 Look carefully at the information on this page and work out what would be the advantages and the disadvantages of living in the cold forest climate.

Gg 1/5b; Gg 2/5a; Gg 3/6b   43

Forecasting the weather

A How a weather forecast is made

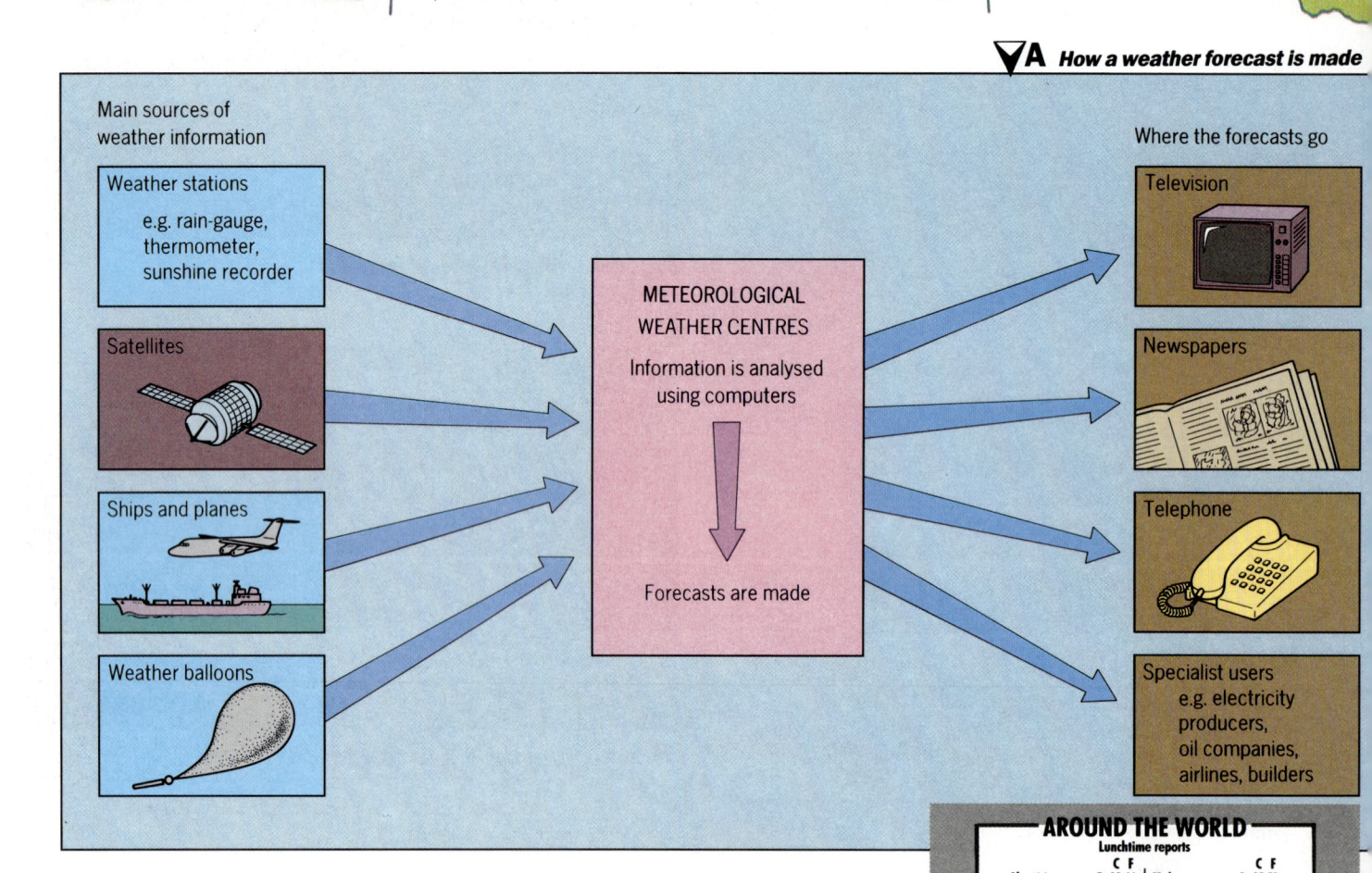

Main sources of weather information:
- Weather stations e.g. rain-gauge, thermometer, sunshine recorder
- Satellites
- Ships and planes
- Weather balloons

METEOROLOGICAL WEATHER CENTRES
Information is analysed using computers
↓
Forecasts are made

Where the forecasts go:
- Television
- Newspapers
- Telephone
- Specialist users e.g. electricity producers, oil companies, airlines, builders

Every day hundreds of weather forecasts are given out all over the world – on TV and radio, in newspapers, over the telephone and through computers (A). In Britain the main centre is the Meteorological Office in Bracknell. There are weather centres elsewhere in the country.

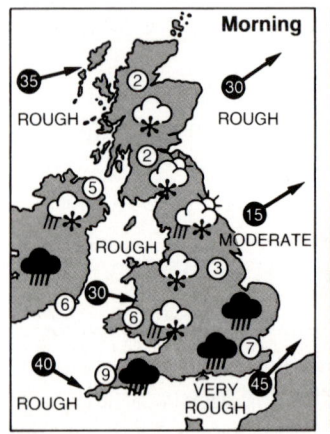

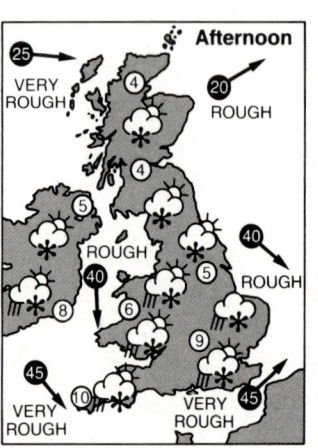

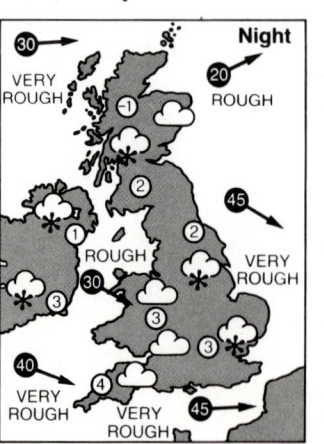

B Many newspapers publish forecasts for Britain . . .

C . . . and world weather information

AROUND THE WORLD
Lunchtime reports

	C F		C F
Akrotiri	F 18 64	Malaga	S 15 59
Algiers	F 16 61	Malta	C 15 59
Amsterdam	C 9 48	Melbourne	R 13 55
Athens	F 15 59	Mexico City	F 18 64
Barbados	C 26 79	Miami	F 27 81
Barcelona	F 12 54	Milan	C 6 43
Belgrade	S 13 55	Moscow	C 0 32
Berlin	S 10 50	New Delhi	S 21 70
Biarritz	F 13 55	New York	C 11 52
Bombay	S 29 84	Nice	C 15 59
Brussels	F 10 50	Palma	R 11 52
Budapest	F 5 41	Paris	F 10 50
Cairo	F 18 64	Peking	S 0 32
Capetown	S 31 88	Perth	S 26 79
Casablanca	F 17 68	Prague	C 4 39
Corfu	S 18 64	Reykjavik	F 2 36
Dubrovnik	F 15 59	Rhodes	S 16 61
Edinburgh	S 6 43	Rome	R 14 57
Faro	S 16 61	San Francisco	S 11 52
Florence	C 16	Seoul	C 0 32
Funchal	C 17 63	Singapore	F 31 88
Geneva	C 9 48	Sydney	R 23 73
Gibraltar	S 15 59	Tangier	C 13 55
Hongkong	C 11 52	Tel Aviv	F 13 55
Innsbruck	F 9 48	Tenerife	S 21 34
Istanbul	C 6 41	Tokyo	Sn 1 34
Johannesburg	F 28 79	Toronto	R 5 41
Karachi	S 22 72	Tunis	F 15 59
Las Palmas	F 20 68	Vancouver	C 1 34
Lisbon	F 14 57	Venice	C 9 48
London	S 9 48	Vienna	C 5 41
Los Angeles	S 14 57	Warsaw	S 8 46
Luxor	S 21 70	Wellington	S 24 75
Madrid	S 7 45	Zurich	S 8 46

S-Sun, F-Fair, C-Cloud, R-Rain, Th-Thunder, Sn-Snow

44

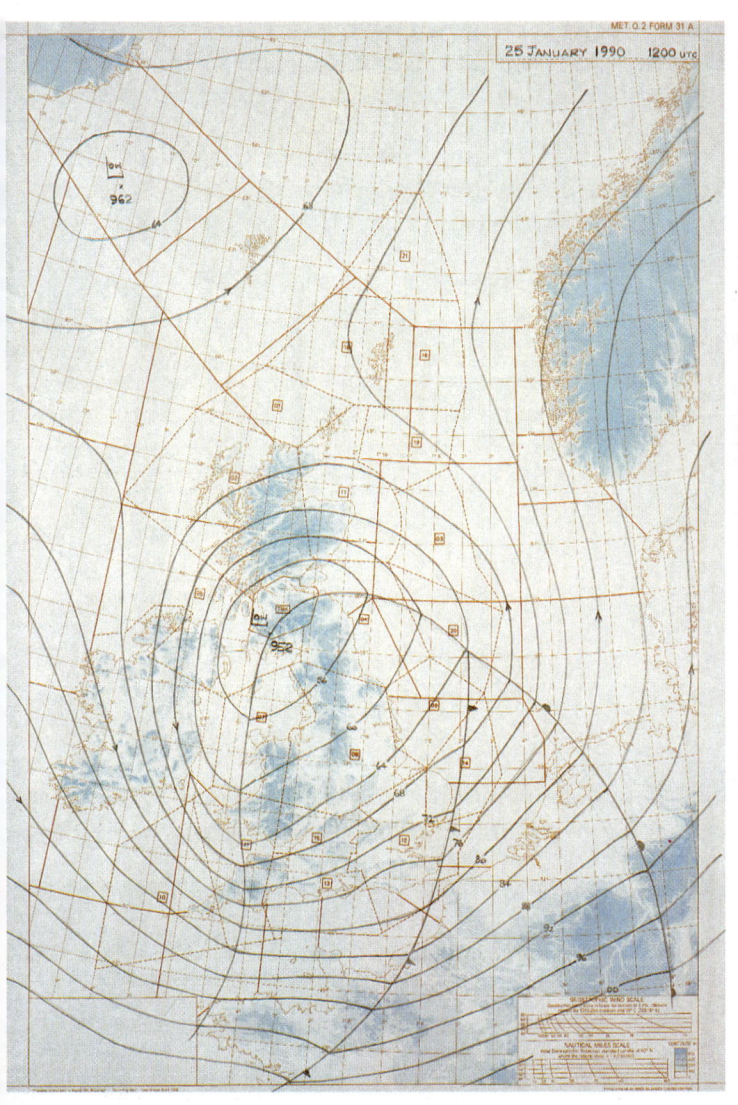

D *Weather chart for 25 January 1990 at 12:00 (midday)*
Crown Copyright

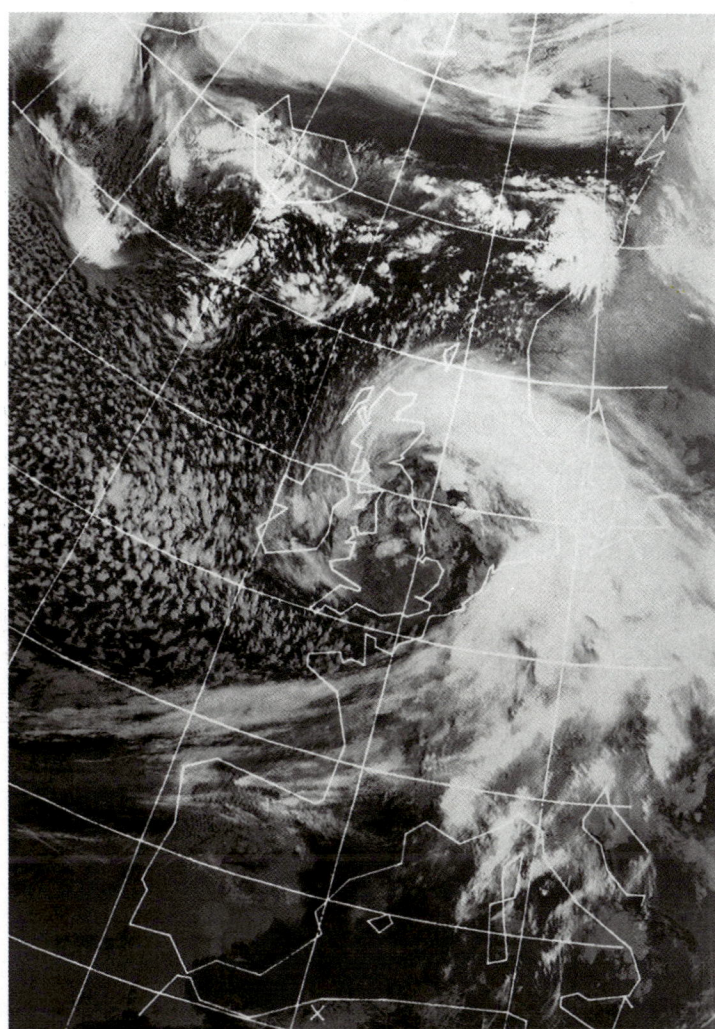

E *Visible image satellite picture taken at approximately 13:00 on 25 January 1990*

Satellites collect information about the **atmosphere** which cannot be gained from ground level. There are two types of satellite picture – visible and infra-red. Visible images show sunlight reflected by the earth (E). Infra-red images show the temperature of the earth's surface.

1 **a** In pairs or small groups make a list of different groups of people who need to listen to the weather forecast, e.g. farmers.
   b For each group suggest reasons why the weather is particularly important to them.

2 **a** Study forecast B and try to work out what each symbol means.
   b Describe in as much detail as possible what the weather was like throughout that day. (D and E also show the same day at 12:00 and 13:00.)

Gg 1/7b, 7c; Gg 3/7a

How the climate changes

Our **climate** is changing all the time but as most of the changes take place over a long time we tend not to notice them. However, there have been examples in the past when a sudden extraordinary event has brought about a climate change. For example, a huge volcanic eruption in Indonesia in 1815 may have had something to do with the fact that the eastern USA and Canada had no summer in 1816 (A–G).

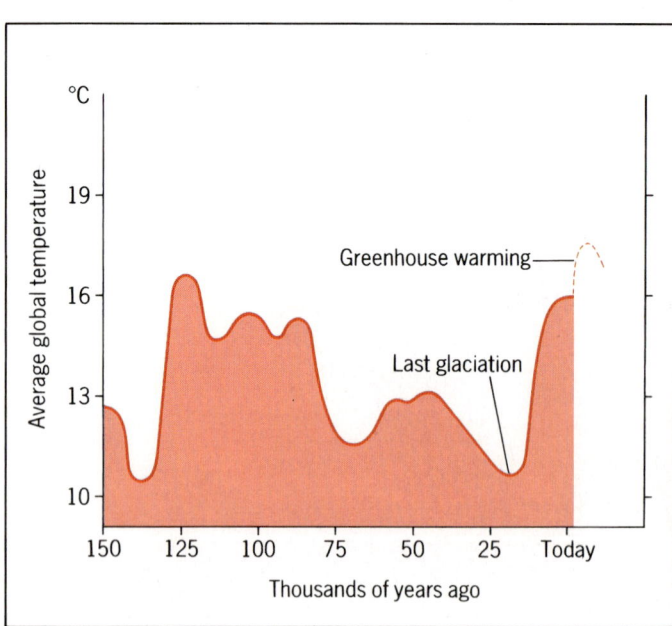

A Historic climate change

B This shows the River Thames frozen over in 1855

The causes of climatic change are very complicated and are thought to include volcanic eruptions (C) and changes in the earth's orbit around the sun.

Many scientists now believe that the '**greenhouse effect**' is causing the earth to warm up (D and E). They predict a rise in temperature of between 2°C and 4°C over the next 50 years. This is called **global warming**. The greenhouse effect describes the build up of certain gases in the **atmosphere** which stop heat from the sun escaping back into space. If the world's temperature does increase there will be many effects, including a rise in sea level (F and G).

C Volcanic eruption

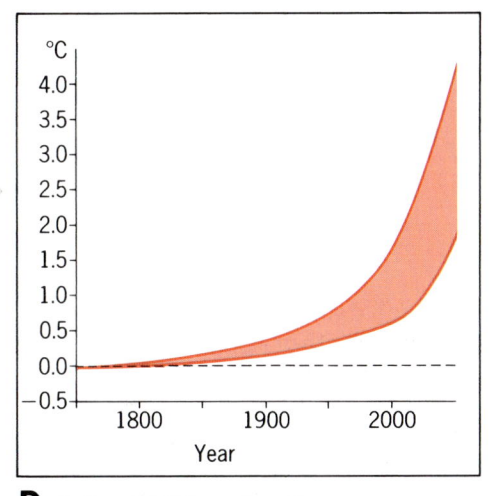

D Estimated future rise of global temperature

E What is the greenhouse effect?

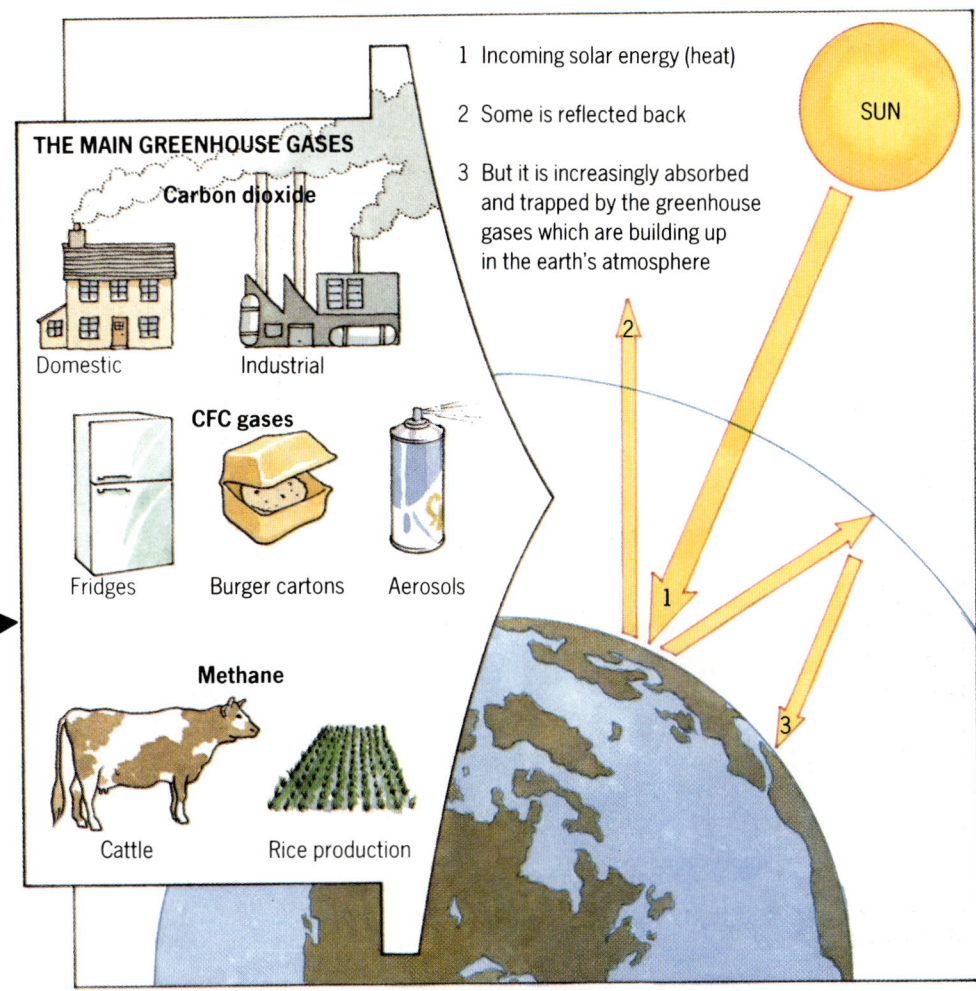

THE MAIN GREENHOUSE GASES

Carbon dioxide — Domestic, Industrial

CFC gases — Fridges, Burger cartons, Aerosols

Methane — Cattle, Rice production

1 Incoming solar energy (heat)

2 Some is reflected back

3 But it is increasingly absorbed and trapped by the greenhouse gases which are building up in the earth's atmosphere

F The effects on humans?

DEPLETED OZONE LAYER
LARGE INCREASES IN SKIN CANCER

SEA LEVEL RISE
SALT CONTAMINATION OF DRINKING WATER, SEWAGE SYSTEM FLOODED, INCREASE IN WATER BORNE DISEASES, ABANDONED SETTLEMENTS

INCREASED DROUGHTS AND OTHER CATASTROPHIC EVENTS, CROP FAILURE, FOOD SHORTAGES AND FAMINE.

HIGHER HEAT AND HUMIDITY
INCREASE IN HEART ATTACKS, INSECT-BORNE DISEASES AND VIOLENCE

G What will happen when the sea level rises?

Areas most at risk from rising sea levels: Dundee, Glasgow, Edinburgh, Tyneside, Carlisle, Middlesbrough, Hull, Liverpool, Towyn, Peterborough, Ipswich, Swansea, Bristol, Southampton, Taunton

1 **a** Estimate how many degrees colder you think it was during the last Ice Age.
b Now use A to work out the actual difference in average temperature between the last Ice Age and today.
c Is it more or less than you originally thought?

2 Describe how your life might be different if the climate in Britain was colder.

3 In pairs, discuss what steps could be taken to help slow down global warming. Draw up a 10-point plan and present it to the rest of the class. Use D and E to help you.

4 Write a newspaper article informing people about the possible effects that global warming could have on them. Use F and G to help you.

Gg 3/6g; Gg 5/7c   47

Glossary

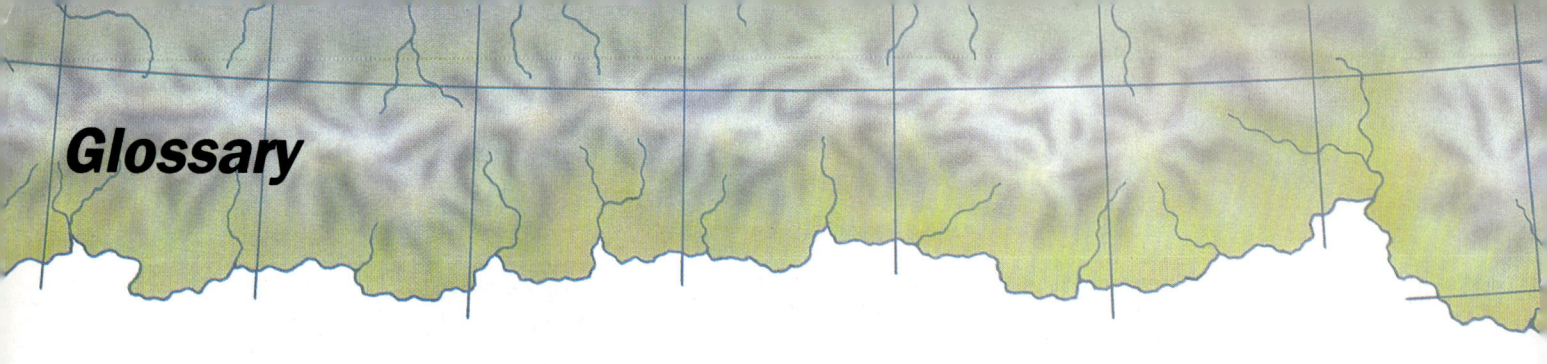

Air masses   large volumes of air which move around the world and bring different types of **weather**
Aspect   direction something faces
Atmosphere   gases surrounding the earth
Catchment area   land around a river system from which water comes into the river
Cirrus   wispy high **clouds**
Climate   average **weather** conditions in a place or area throughout the **seasons**
Cloud   mass of visible moisture in the sky
Condensation level   height in the sky where **clouds** form
Condense   change from gas to liquid (water vapour cools and turns into water droplets)
Confluence   junction of two rivers
Convection   the way air rises because of warmth below it
Cumulus   heaped **cloud**
Deposition   putting down of **transported** material
Desert   very dry area with low and unreliable rainfall
Drainage basin   area drained by a river system
Equator   line of 0° **latitude** midway between North and South **Poles**
Erosion   wearing away of the land's surface
Evaporate   change from liquid to gas (water is warmed and turns into water vapour)
Flash flood   sudden flood after heavy rainfall in the **desert**
Front   where two air masses meet
Global warming   increase in **temperatures** around the world
Greenhouse effect   build up of certain gases in the **atmosphere** which stops heat from the sun from escaping back into space
Hurricane   severe tropical storm with heavy rain and violent winds
Impermeable   surface that does not allow water to sink in
Infiltration   process of water sinking into the ground
Interception   process of stopping water from reaching the ground, e.g. by trees or plants

Latitude   lines around the earth drawn parallel to the **Equator**, measured in degrees North or South of the **Equator**
Meander   river bend
Microclimate   climate of a small area, e.g. a garden or room
Mouth   where a river flows into the sea
Nimbus   rain **cloud**
North Atlantic Drift   warm ocean current from the Gulf of Mexico which flows across the Atlantic and past the north west of Britain
Permeable   surface that allows water to sink in and pass through
Plunge pool   deep pool at the foot of a **waterfall** made by the swirling action of water and rocks
Poles   extreme points of the Earth, North and South, farthest from the **Equator**
Precipitation   water, in any form, that falls from the sky, e.g. rain, snow, hail and dew
Pressure   force that air exerts
Resort   town that attracts holidaymakers
Runoff   water that flows over land into streams
Satellite   instrument that collects information about the **atmosphere** from above ground level
Saturated air   air full of water vapour
Seasons   times of the year when there are differences in average **temperatures** and hours of sunlight
Stratus   large horizontal sheet **cloud**
Thermometer   instrument for measuring **temperature**
Thermometer screen   standard shelter to keep a **thermometer** shaded
Transportation   carrying of material from one place to another
Waterfall   sudden fall of water over a step or ledge in a river bed
Weather   conditions in the **atmosphere** such as **temperatures** and **precipitation**